Through the Darkness

Through the Darkness

Coping with the Legacy of Mental Illness

Eleanor L Futscher

Writers Club Press

San Jose New York Lincoln Shanghai

Through the Darkness
Coping with the Legacy of Mental Illness

Writers Club Press
an imprint of iUniverse.com, Inc.

For information address:
iUniverse.com, Inc.
620 North 48th Street, Suite 201
Lincoln, NE 68504-3467
www.iuniverse.com

ISBN: 0-595-12759-2

Printed in the United States of America

For my husband Roy.

Preface

In my life I have learned a lot about mental illness. Growing up with a mentally ill father, struggling to maintain my own stability, then having our son diagnosed with schizophrenia, I have been compelled to look at what we call mental illness. I have thought a lot about an aspect of mental illness that was rarely addressed by professionals when discussing Mark's case.

I have heard the theory that "malevolent mothering" causes schizophrenia and more recently that genes are at fault. In the years when we were dealing with Mark's illness, the prevailing opinion of leading psychologists and psychiatrists was that the mother was guilty of faulty parenting when a child became mentally ill. A highly respected therapist, Bruno Bettelheim, was an advocate of this theory. Many professionals followed his lead, some going so far as to take the child out of the home into their own.

I do not wish to argue long or hard against either of those theories. Instead I should like to add one of my own, that of personal responsibility. Since I have lived in the shadow of mental illness all my life, I have learned that it is nurtured by the personal choices the afflicted person makes in spite of efforts to direct him or her to more health-affirming activity.

Watching our son as his illness progressed, I noticed he was making more and more destructive choices which I am convinced, on some level, he knew were wrong. As these choices grew in number, he got in deeper trouble until he had dug so deep a trough that he could no longer extricate himself. His life became so mixed up it literally "drove him crazy".

Each time we make a choice that violates our ethics and our integrity, conscious or unconscious, it works against us. In the case of the mentally ill person, I believe many choices are unconscious. It is a well-known fact that the manic-depressive person has very poor judgment, which compromises his or her ability to visualize consequences. Each destructive action makes the next one easier until the point of no return is reached. Finally, the disease is so great that it manifests in disease. When we violate our integrity and ethics over time, we may lose our health.

Chapter I

All night I tossed, sleeplessly waiting for day to break. When morning came I rose to a foggy overcast world, typical of our spring mornings in Northern California. My mood was even heavier than the fog that greeted my rising. The house was cold, and as I reached for my robe I shivered. I looked at my husband Roy still sleeping in bed.

"It's time to get up," I said. "We're due at the hospital at ten." He groaned and turned over. Irritated by his response, I walked away from the bed. I looked listlessly in my closet. I was tired and discouraged, and it was hard to care what I wore or how I looked.

This was the day that Roy and I were going to the mental hospital to confer with the doctor and staff about our son, Mark. A foreboding sense of doom hung like a shroud around me. What would I hear at the hospital? Would they have some avenues for us to pursue? Where would we place our son? Did anyone have the skills and the knowledge to help us? Would the new breakthroughs in psychopharmacology be available to him and be effective in his case? The questions rattling around in my head were endless. I hoped to find some answers today.

Though it had been some weeks, I was still shocked by what had happened. I did not really believe it. I kept thinking that I would go to sleep and wake up to find it had only been a nightmare. In my waking state, I only wanted for the day to end so that I could sleep and forget that I had not been dreaming. This last sleepless night was like many before. It had been some time since I had slept peacefully. I was worried and agitated night and day.

As I prepared breakfast, I listened for Roy's footsteps. I wondered why I even bothered with food. Neither of us would feel like eating. I put the glass of juice down as Roy entered the room. I wondered what he was feeling. His face was drawn. He looked older than his fifty-three years. I barely heard his soft greeting as he sat down to eat. I wanted to talk to still the anxiety I was feeling but I could tell that he did not want to converse. We said very little, each in our own thoughts. I wondered what his were. If I could wonder about him, I wouldn't have to think about my own depressing fears.

When we spoke, our words were a rehash of our individual foreboding, things we had heard each other say before. We were running out of ideas. We talked to still the voices that planted fears, doubts and anxiety. Things were out of control and we were helpless to change them. It was frightening.

I looked at my watch, eager to be on the way. I gathered my things to leave while Roy went back upstairs for the car keys. These familiar habits reminded me that our life had form, that some things were not out of control.

As we drove I put a tape in the tape deck. Tapes of the seventies played songs that we had heard Mark playing when he was a student living at home. Tears streamed down my face as we made our way across the San Francisco Bay Bridge. I tried to wipe them away as inconspicuously as possible, before Roy could see that I was crying again. I was ashamed of how much I cried over our son. The tears would not be stopped. Before we got to the hospital, I felt that I had to get control of myself. I did not want the hospital staff to see me as an overly emotional woman, to think of me as unstable. Besides, I was beginning to be ashamed of how much I cried, and how easily.

I looked over at my husband. His jaw was set. His eyes looked straight ahead on the road before him. I could tell that he was trying to hold back his tears. There were no comforting words we could give each other.

I wanted to be calm when we talked with the doctors so that they would listen to what I had to say. I had heard their potential diagnosis of schizophrenia, one that I refused to accept. I was prepared to refute the diagnosis with my knowledge and experience. I knew a lot about mental illness. I had lived in its shadow all my life and psychology was my field of interest and study. Roy and I were experienced in the counseling field. They would see that I was a knowledgeable woman, that I had an opinion worth hearing.

When we arrived at the psychiatric wing of the hospital we rang for admittance. While we waited, I felt my throat tighten. I wanted to turn and run. Never did a hospital offer me less hope or comfort. This was the end of the line for our son Mark, a psychiatric hospital. What were we doing here? What was Mark doing here? How did we come to this? How were we going to get help? Where? So many questions. Up to now there had been no answers,

I brought a pair of Mark's favorite tennis shoes, carrying the box under my arm. He was wearing flimsy hospital slippers. His shoes had been lost at the county hospital, from where he had been transferred, where possessions were regularly lost or stolen. Mark was sitting rigid on the edge of his bed when I entered his room with the shoes. It was near Easter time.

" I brought you an Easter present," I said. I tried to smile. He looked so forlorn that the half-formed smile died before it had a chance. I put my arms around him. His rigid body softened. He broke into wrenching sobbing. We couldn't have spoken, we were both crying so much.

We sat down. I looked him over. He was so thin. In a short time he had shrunk from a husky healthy young twenty-two-year old man to a near skeleton. He had not been eating since he had come to this hospital and was now being force-fed. Earlier I had spoken to the doctor about the force-feeding when he had told me of Mark's refusal to eat. I don't know what prompted me to say it, and I wondered if the doctor was shocked:

"If he doesn't want to eat, why don't you just let him be? He has a right to die if he chooses that. Maybe he knows something we don't know," I had said.

Did I have a premonition of what his fate was going to be? I think I did. I had been down this lane before with my father's lifelong struggle with mental illness. Did I want him to choose death over that fate for himself as well as for me? Yes, an unequivocal yes! I did! I was selfish to wish for the easy solution. I was thinking only of myself.

The doctor had a rational medical answer, "Of course we can't let him die. It is only his illness that makes him want to die. If he were in a different state, he would want to live."

How dumb did he think I am? That goes without saying. I was angry with his cool clinical attitude. I wanted him to appreciate how much I was hurting. His reply inflamed my ready anger. I wondered if the doctors were doing Mark or anyone else a service by forcing him to live against his will. How was Mark's case different from all those cases of persons being kept on life-support machines long after their brain/mind died? What difference if it is body or the mind that is no longer functioning? Was Mark doomed to a living death? Would he want that? I don't know. Much later I came to realize that the gift of life is the most precious thing we have, that whatever one's state, it is natural to want to live. To wish it to end for someone else is a grave travesty. There undoubtedly was a part of Mark that did want to live.

The doctor had gone on, "You know he tried to commit suicide once already here." When he began to describe what Mark had done, I stopped him. I did not want to hear it. There are some things too hard to hear. I had known before that Mark had strong suicidal tendencies. His driving off a cliff at 115 miles an hour prior to his first hospitalization at age twenty-one had been construed as a suicide attempt. Sometime later in his illness Mark told me with a hopeless tone in a mood of dark despair, "Mom, I can't even kill myself!"

After we visited privately with Mark, we were summoned to the day room to confer with the staff. The sun had broken through the fog. As I looked out the window, I could see a whole world of normal activity outside these walls inside which everything around me appeared distorted and unreal.

Seated in the conference room were the two nurses, and the doctor. Roy asked about what treatment procedures were being followed, what drugs were being used. We learned that Mark was in seclusion most of the time he had been in the hospital. When I asked what that meant, the nurse explained, "Mark becomes wild, destructive to himself, beats his head on the floor, tears at his skin and tries anything he can think of to harm himself. We put him in a padded room and restrain him physically to protect him from himself. We keep constant watch on him."

I felt sick. I was learning more about hospital procedure than I cared to hear. I would like to have walked out. I felt my body tense as I watched the doctor. When my father was ill with depression I tried to shut out what happened by not looking too closely. As a child, I would not have been able to make sense out of his illness. Ironically, as an adult I was no more successful in making sense out of Mark's illness. I would try to understand and help Mark. I would not run away this time.

The doctor asked us if we would like Mark to join us for part of our discussion.

When we said we would, the doctor asked Roy to bring Mark in. When Roy stood up to leave the doctor said, "Your son is very ill."

I had hoped to hear some words of encouragement. I began to fear what he would say next. Roy went across the hall and returned with Mark. The doctor looked at the nurses and then across the room to us. I could tell that they were hedging, not wanting to tell us what they knew we would not want to hear.

"We think you need to know. Your son has been diagnosed as a para-noid schizophrenic," the doctor was calm. "Most difficult to treat and with very poor prognosis," he added.

Speechless, I stared while everything around me blurred. I felt alone in this room of people. If there were a crueler phrase in the English language, it would have to be one I had never heard. My mouth went dry. When I tried to swallow, I felt as if I was going to choke. If he had said they just dropped the atom bomb on Berkeley, I would have felt no more shock or more helplessness. I knew enough about psychology and mental illness to know that there could be no more damning diagnosis.

Roy was silent. When I was able to speak, I said, "You're wrong. If he has to have a diagnosis at this point, it would be manic-depressive."

I knew about manic-depressive. I could handle that. They had to change their minds and would when they heard me out.

"Oh, no, you're wrong," I repeated. "I know this boy. He is my son. I have watched him for some time. I have known things were not right with him. He has been hyperactive for months, even years, but that is only because he is running away from his depressive side. When you begin to work with him further, you will uncover his depression."

I became brilliant in my confidence that I was right. When they saw I knew about their field, they would listen to me. They would have to with-draw that outrageous label before our son believed them, too.

I turned to the nurse, "Do you agree with that diagnosis?" My incredu-lous tone would further convince her that it was ridiculous to entertain such a diagnosis. I could see that this sensible woman would accept it as I saw it and dare to challenge the doctor with the real truth.

Her simple, "Yes," shattered any remaining arguments I might have had.

Mark shifted in his chair. Roy looked at me before he spoke. I cannot remember what he said though his voice was calm and factual. I wondered how he could be so calm when I was feeling like the bottom had dropped out of my world. I went numb. I couldn't feel another thing. I was already on overload as I looked at Mark's confused expression.

I remembered staff meetings at our counseling service where diagnoses were made. When there was a suggestion that the client might have schizophrenic tendencies, our staff psychiatrist remarked, "They are the most difficult to treat. Unlike the manic-depressives, who are charming and easy to talk with, these patients make your skin crawl sometimes. You can't reach them."

But now, I said to myself, "I don't believe it! I will never accept that diagnosis. I don't care what kind of behavior they are seeing. Mark is not a schizophrenic!"

Prior to this diagnosis, I had kept quiet about the mental illness in my family fearful it would prejudice the medics in their assessment. Now that I did not like what they were saying I decided they needed to hear about my father.

"Let me tell you about my father. It could shed some light on Mark's case." I said.

"Oh, we don't need any family history. There is no doubt that your son is schizophrenic." The doctor was adamant.

Mark had been brought into the hospital at age twenty-two in a delusional state a week before we now saw him but had been having delusions for sometime. It is difficult to target a time since we did not realize how much was going on inside his head that later became recognizable as delusional. He did not behave like a manic-depressive. Small wonder. He had not been sleeping for days. He had been seriously disturbed for months. About a year previous to his hospitalization, Mark had come to his father for help in finding a psychotherapist. Roy and I had been urging Mark to seek help for months. Mark was a workaholic, racing around from job to job until he was unable to sleep night or day. Things began to go badly in his painting business. He was not keeping his commitments to his customers. He stopped attending classes at the University of California, and at the same time he increased his activities at an alarming rate. He took on more work than he could do, joined a yacht club and registered at two colleges at once. Though he wasn't living at home, I knew what was going on since he came by the house regularly. I knew that Mark just needed to slow down. If he were treated for depression, he had a chance of recovering his health. I was no doctor, but I had experience and was sure that I knew what I was talking about. I would find someone who would listen to me.

I wanted to get out of that hospital. As soon as we could comfortably take our leave, we said good-bye to Mark, thanked the staff and left. I wanted to talk to my husband who would be as hopeful as I that they would change their minds about the diagnosis.

Roy had worked in hospitals all of his career. When we first met he was spending a summer at a state mental hospital working as a ward attendant. For years he had visited and counseled on psychiatric wards. As we drove home, I asked, "You don't believe them, do you?" He didn't answer me. His eyes were riveted to the road. Tears were falling into his lap. Through sobs he said, "Let's go home."

My God, he did believe them! I was mute until we arrived home. We went into the living room. I lay down on the floor and sobbed. Roy dropped down beside me. We held each other and cried. We had no words. We were losing our first-born son. For a moment, I didn't want to live the pain. Life was too bleak for words. I cried until I was drained of all energy and motivation. I felt as if I would never be able to go on again. Suddenly as I had dropped to the floor, I sat up.

"This will never do. We have to come to our senses. It won't change a thing if we lay here and cry until doomsday," I said. I felt grounded as I uttered the words aloud. My reason returned. "I have college work to do and you have a doctoral program to finish." I felt strong and in charge of myself. I would help Roy, and we would pull ourselves together and go on with our lives.

Roy sat up. We began to talk about our situation. We spoke of the need to go on with confidence and faith in the future. We had three other grown children who needed us. None of us were ill. It was our son that was ill: his cruel fate, not ours. We could not give up for the sake of the rest of our children and ourselves.

If I could have envisioned the cruelest fate that could befall my child, I would have picked the one that fell to Mark's lot. Even before I knew what we would all go through together, I was afraid. Would I be strong enough to stand the tests? How would I keep my stability? For the first time in my life, I had been fully free of the burdens of the past only to have thrust upon me a heavier burden than I had borne thus far. If Mark's diagnosis had been manic-depressive would he be recovering his health today? Would he have had a different destiny? Maybe. It makes no difference now. There are no second chances.

These and other thoughts formed in my mind as over months and years I tried to make sense out of the tragedy that struck our close family and rent it apart. Along with Mark's illness, my childish dreams of living happily ever after vanished. I would never again be "happy" in the way that I had believed in for so many years as a happily married woman, mother of four healthy children.

My chance for happiness now lies in accepting what is, not what might have been.

Chapter II.

As a child of immigrant parents, I felt pulled between my German heritage and my American birth. At the same time, I was pulled toward loyalty toward Russia, my parents' homeland. My parents were Germans living in Russia. When they were newly weds they came to the United States. In 1911 they settled on a North Dakota farm. Years later when I was born, the third youngest in a family of ten children, my parents were Americanized and did not speak much of their homeland. I knew only that my father was an orphan and had been in the Czar's army. Neither of my parents went beyond the fourth grade. They were both determined that their children should be educated. We did not disappoint them.

My father had been a manic-depressive who had to go in and out of the mental hospital throughout my growing years. When he was depressed, which was often, it would be the task of the children to get him up in the morning. Mother would try to get him up and fail. Then she would send one of my older sisters in to try. My sister would fail then I would be sent in. A little girl, not more than five the first time I can remember it happening, I stood beside his bed, hopeful that his love for me would get him to respond. He promised me he would get up and then he did not do so. I went in again.

"Dad, you promised to get up. Now get up!" I would order in my childish voice. Sometimes I would be crying. As it happened more and more, I became discouraged by his stubbornness. At the same time I was left with doubt about myself. Maybe there was something I wasn't doing right, something I didn't know about that would have worked. There didn't seem any good reason why my father couldn't get up if he wanted to. He didn't seem sick and talked to me when I came into his room.

The seeds of low self-esteem and helplessness were sown then and took root in me in those years as I watched my father struggle with his own feelings of worthlessness and shame. Many times I heard him say, "I'm no good. You'd all be better off without me."

It seemed that when he was depressed, the hardest thing was for him to get up in the morning. If he was able to get himself up, as the day progressed he would feel better and better and by evening he seemed almost normal. The next morning, however, it would start all over again. Some days he would not get up at all. Other days, with encouragement and sometimes of his own volition, he would get up even when he was depressed.

My father would be able to work on the farm for periods of time following a depressive period. After a while he would become hyperactive and move into the manic phase. In this phase he was more unpredictable. He would work at a feverish pitch to make up for lost time until he would be so energized he could not sleep. He would talk and act wildly. He would threaten to kill himself then would disappear, if we did not watch him closely or follow him. When we could not find him we would look in the kitchen drawer for the large knife used for butchering. When dad was missing mother would always open the knife drawer before she went to look for him. I wonder if he told her that is what he would use or had tried to kill himself with a knife. I had re-occurring nightmares about that large knife when I was a child.

When it became impossible to watch him night and day or to restrain him physically, we would have to have him hospitalized. Sometimes my brother would take him to the hospital. He used to get homesick whenever he was in the hospital, far from home where the family could not visit him often. One time he was too wild to be trusted in the car as he was resisting being taken from home. The sheriff was called. He came with a deputy, handcuffed my father and took him away. I was shocked and sad. I wanted to scream, "He's not a criminal. He's my father. Don't take him away!" There was no one to speak to about what I was feeling. It was early morning. I went off to the woods alone. I was too hurt and bewildered to cry. I couldn't make sense out of what had happened and it was not talked about in my family. We did not easily share tender or hurt feelings with one another. Maybe everyone was so relieved to have the stress removed and our father safe that we didn't want to think about him for a while. That made it hard for me to admit how much I missed my father. Our fatherless family had all it could do to keep going on a large farm already short of manpower.

Years later, in a dream, I relived the scene of my father being taken away in handcuffs. I told my mother the dream, and then I said, "Mother, I don't think as a child I had the capacity to experience the depth of grief and anguish I felt." We cried together. We could talk then long after my father was gone.

There were many scenes like the one of the little girl standing beside the bed pleading with her father to get up. Writing about it years later I can feel the hopelessness of that little girl, when, through the years, her father did not get better. I felt like a fatherless child. One blue day, years later, I wrote in my journal.

"He was wrapped in his illness, warmly encased in his cocoon of disease so that my earliest memories were of having to take care of him. My father couldn't take care of me and I learned not to expect him to do so.

When I was about seven I remember nearly choking to death coughing. Mother did not hear from downstairs. The coughing persisted until I heard the door open. My older brother, who rarely showed affection for me, came in my room. 'Here, suck on this,' he said tenderly as he handed me a cough drop. It is one of the few intimate fatherly acts I recall gratefully from childhood."

My father's illness followed me all the days of my youth. I was not a happy child. When I look at the pictures taken of me when I was a girl, I seldom see a smile. I remember being accused by my older sister of "always frowning." What was there to smile about? I was a worried child.

While it seems to me now that he was more depressed than manic, it is possible I was less aware of his manic phases because he would have to be hospitalized when he became hyperactive, while when he was depressed we could take care of him at home. He was gone for long periods of time during my childhood.

In the beginning of his manic phases, he would be cheerful with high energy and exuding confidence. He was productive for a time then became overactive and did foolish things. He bought land he could not afford, lent money to people who did not pay him back, worked himself into a frenzy by his inability to slow down and would soon become irrational and dangerous to himself. He would have to be hospitalized during these phases.

For years I prayed for him to recover. I asked God to help him and wished he could do more to help himself. It was not until our son had been ill many years that I realized that both he and my father had little control over their lives. They were each in a whirlwind buffeted about by emotions they did not understand, were unable to control, victims of a tragically debilitating disease.

By the time I went to high school I think I had come to terms with the fact that my father was never going to recover. Proficient in watching out for him, I was sensitive to his moods. I was fourteen that summer. One night we were going to a young people's meeting at church and Dad was going to be left alone. I went to tell him we were going. Though he had not been getting up those days, by evening he sometimes would feel better and talk. This evening he seemed more despondent than usual.

"Don't leave me alone," he pleaded.

"But I want to go with the others," I argued. He begged. I felt guilty for wanting to go more than to take care of him.

"If you go, I'll kill myself," he threatened. In the past, this threat would have been sufficient to make me change my plans instantly. Something was different this time.

"Well, then kill yourself, I'm not going to stay home and take care of you the rest of my life."

My boldness surprised him as much as it did me. His eyes opened wide. His face became animated. I saw a faint smile play at his mouth. Looking directly at me he said quietly, "You go, I'll be all right. I just said that so you wouldn't leave me alone. I won't do anything foolish," I believed him. We left him alone and he was asleep when we returned that night. From that time on I no longer feared that he would harm himself. I knew his secret. His threats were a way to manipulate mother and the rest of us.

In his loneliness, he had learned cunning ways to get attention. He hid from us, threatened to kill himself, bemoaned his worthlessness until he had us all feeling worse than he. At the same time as he pushed us away, he also begged us not to desert him. If Mother were not around the house, he would anxiously inquire about her. When he came in from the fields, his first question was, "Where's mother?" I suppose she was his link to a sane world. Through all the years of living with this man, she kept her steadiness. She was a strong loving woman. Until my father died at sixty-five, she took care of him. Even with her loving support, she was unable to save him from his fate. He never recovered but died of a heart attack in the mental hospital.

I used to envy children who spoke of their fathers with pride. I was ashamed of my father and did not want to talk about him. I hoped people wouldn't ask about him. If he had been ill with a weak heart, we could have admitted it without shame. Even cancer could be talked about but mental illness was a damning condition and not always considered a disease. People did not admit to having a family member who was crazy. If it were possible they would hide them away. Though everyone knew about my father, especially when he had been taken to the hospital, we could pretend they didn't know if we didn't talk about it. Only when the children at school taunted us with having a crazy father did we suffer the humiliation publicly that we felt privately.

Where I grew up in North Dakota in a large farm family, I was lucky for the opportunity to finish high school. Many farm boys and girls stayed on the farm, never going beyond eighth grade. College was considered a waste for girls. They were expected to marry and leave home. Those that did not marry stayed home with their families on the farm.

From my early years I had dreams of going to college. I knew they were dreams I personally would have to make come true, as there would be little or no financial support from home. After graduation from high school, I took a job in a factory where I worked for a year to save money for college. The next year I enrolled at the University of Minnesota with plans to become a social worker.

The University was exciting and stimulating to me after coming from a quiet farm community with few cultural or intellectual opportunities. Though I was not able to participate fully in University life because of my outside job, I still enjoyed being in the University setting, and I was proud to be taking care of myself, independent of my parents.

After two years, however, the stress of job and school were too much for me. I dropped out of school to earn money to continue later in college. I got a job at a furnace company where I met a young man who was working as a furnace installer. We began to date. It was good to have time for dates and money to spend for things other than books. I almost forgot that I wanted to finish college. I became engaged and made plans to marry Jim.

Jim was good and kind and promised to provide well for me if I married him. After ordering my dress and dresses for the bridesmaids and finalizing plans for the house we were going to build, I realized that I did not want to marry Jim. He was a high school graduate with no interest in intellectual matters. I don't think he ever read a book after high school. We could never have lived happily together; our goals were different. I was as greedy for knowledge as he was for making a good living and having a secure financial base. It was the financial security, which I had never had, that was the bait that nearly seduced me into a marriage that would surely have been an unhappy one for me. After living at the poverty level through high school and college, I temporarily lost sight of my personal goals when I was offered an easier path.

Books and education have always been important to me and college was a life-long goal. I knew that I would want to get back to college again soon. Jim would not be sympathetic to that desire. Though I was reluctant to break off the engagement for fear that I would never meet another man to marry, I knew I could not go through with the marriage. While I did want marriage and children I also wanted a college education. With trepidation, I took my chances and broke off with Jim. I would not marry just to marry. He did not accept the break-up easily. He was hurt and bewildered, but I was relieved.

About two weeks later, I was walking down the street talking and laughing with a friend. I was feeling light and relieved over my broken engagement, not missing Jim or worrying about another date as I thought I might.

Roy was riding the streetcar home when he spied me on the street and decided to ask me out. Apparently he had noticed me at the Lutheran Student meetings I had attended at the University when I could find time. He looked up my phone number and called me. He was not dating anyone at the time so he asked what I was doing and would I like to go out?

We began seeing each other every day. He invited me to a fraternity party where I met his friends. In only a few weeks we realized that we were in love with each other and talked about marrying. I could hardly believe my good fortune. To have found someone compatible so soon seemed like a dream. Roy was well educated, kind, handsome, and skilled with his hands, but above all, I knew he would be a good father. I wanted my children to have the steadiness of a father. Roy would provide a masculine authority I had missed growing up. The gods were kind to me when they brought us together. I shudder when I think of how close we came to not meeting.

It was only three months after we began dating that we were married. I did not return to college but took a job while Roy finished seminary in Minneapolis then did another year of graduate study. I settled into nest building forgetting my plans for finishing college. That would come later.

Both of us wanted children. As soon as Roy was ready for a call to a parish we started our family. We settled in Waterloo, Wisconsin. In the two years before our first child we had gotten to know and enjoy each other. Those were the most carefree times I had ever known. When they ended I was ready for family responsibilities.

Thrilled with my first pregnancy, we planned for a boy. Like most of the population, we wanted a boy first. I was confident that I would have daughters, too. We planned for six children. Two people as happy as we ought to have lots of children to share their love.

The first picture I purchased for the baby's room was one of a little boy kneeling for his evening prayers. I planned the nursery for a boy. Before that picture found a place on the wall and the nursery would be occupied by a son, I bore two girls.

The Reed Method of natural childbirth was new at the time of my first pregnancy. I decided to do the exercises and have my child by that method. Though I did the exercises only a few months prior to her birth, my labor was three hours, the easiest one of the four. We barely made it to the hospital where I watched, fully conscious and awake during her birth. We were so thrilled to be parents of a healthy child, Beth, we forgot we had ever wanted a boy.

Though it was earlier than we had planned, when a year later I was pregnant once again, we were happy. The first pregnancy had been so easy that I did not dread another so soon on the heels of the first. I itched night and day from the onset of pregnancy until I gave birth. We were never able to find out the cause. I was exhausted most of the time as it was impossible to sleep soundly for those nine months. Our second daughter, Deborah, another healthy girl, was born to us.

I was busy with two children now, able to care for them and enjoy life with my husband and in the parish in a small town where he was the pastor. By the time Mark arrived, less than two years later, we were experienced parents.

Mark was a January baby born in the Midwest. The night we went to the hospital the temperature had dropped below zero. The snow was crisp beneath our feet. The sky was dense with stars. We shivered with cold and excitement. This could be our boy. My labor was easy and soon over. The doctor had arranged for Roy to attend the birth, a practice not often approved in those days. We were able to convince the doctor that Roy would behave very well as he had worked in and been around the hospital setting during his pastoral training. What happiness prevailed in that delivery room when I was delivered of a healthy boy! His father held him before I did. The doctor handed the child to his father whose broad smile assured me that we couldn't have done better.

Mark's arrival cooperated nicely with our schedule. It was early Sunday morning when he arrived allowing his father to get back to his duties at the church. The highlight of the announcements that day was Mark's birth.

"My what a proud man he was that morning, Eleanor. You should have seen his smiling face. We would have known even if he hadn't told us. And his having a son made it ever so special for pastor," one of my friends from the parish told me later.

We settled in, now a family of five. We had three children under four years old. I was content to stop having children for a time. The people in the parish were supportive and kind. I did not feel burdened by the daily care of the family. I had always had to work from the time I was small so that the work did not seem as overwhelming as people used to think it was. When I went to high school, I worked for my room and board with a family with two children. My last year of high school I held a part-time job. To earn money for college I had a job thirty hours a week while attending the university full time. So when people said, "How do you take care of all those little ones?" I didn't understand what they were talking about. I felt taken care of with a good husband and security such as I had not known before.

Though we had some frightening times with the children, these were generally stress-free years. One afternoon my husband was working at the church a few doors down from our home, a river ran behind our house and the church, with a fence in need of repair, separating our house from the river. I was working at home one afternoon when my husband came running into the house, breathless. His white face held a look of terror. I felt my stomach knot. Something was wrong.

"Beth's drowned," he gasped.

He was wrong. Beth was upstairs taking her afternoon nap. He must have wondered why I was so calm.

"I saw her straw hat floating down the river," he said. "She must have gotten through the broken fence and fallen in the river." Now my stomach did a double knot. She was beginning to climb out of her crib. Maybe she got out. Together we charged up the stairs, two at a time, Roy nearly knocking me down as he pushed me out of the way. With thankfulness and relief we gazed down at our peacefully sleeping child. We made sure that the fence was repaired that week.

When I found time on my hands I joined the League of Women Voters so as to meet people apart from my husband's work. I registered for a night course to further my degree program. I was haunted by a vague restlessness, which I tried to assuage by increasing my knowledge. In my psychology courses I used my children for subjects. In the role of observer,

I further appreciated what wonderful fragile beings children are. Naive in my enthusiasm for participating in politics, I engaged in a campaign to recall Senator Joseph McCarthy in our little town of pro-McCarthy supporters. My husband received a letter from the church council asking him to ask me to "refrain from politics." I was incensed that they did not communicate directly with me. I was on the way to becoming an independent liberated woman.

We began plans to move out of the parish ministry. Roy shared my desire to live in a large metropolitan area. His interest lay in integrating psychology and religion. My interests were similar though for personal reasons rather than professional. I was reared in the church and valued its teachings yet I found the hard questions I had were sometimes better addressed and answered by psychology. My lifetime interest became "making sense out of life through understanding of psychology and the experience of religion." Though Roy and I were very different in temperament, we shared the same basic values. Through trying times, this was an anchor, which kept us steady and together.

While the parish was an easy happy place for our family, we were anxious to move to a large city for more training and intellectual stimulation. I was itching to get back into the classroom. To work as a chaplain, Roy was to have four years of parish experience. Before the four years were up, there was a job opportunity on the West Coast. We were invited to Green Bay, Wisconsin, about sixty miles from our parish, to an interview. After the interview Roy was asked to finish out the year in the parish, then go to California for further training to set up a hospital chaplaincy program in pastoral clinical education, one of the first programs of its kind on the West Coast. We were thrilled that the job was in Berkeley, California.

Before Mark was a year old, we said good-bye to our dear friends and family and moved across the country where Roy would have a position commensurate with his talent and interests. I would be able to pursue my education at the University in Berkeley. My plans to become a social worker had been put on hold. Now they would become a reality in a university town where there were ample opportunities for classes. Though I was content in my role as a homemaker and mother, I planned to have more time for myself as the children grew. I never wavered in my faith that I could do my job at home and have a career in due time. I held onto that dream long after reality dictated a different destiny.

When we left a blinding snowstorm in Wisconsin in late November, we found sunshine and summer temperatures in California. We were ecstatic with our new life in this wonderful new state where the children could play outside without snowsuits or jackets in November. I laughed when I saw the neighbor children playing barefoot outside on the coldest winter day.

Our children were healthy although they had the usual childhood illnesses. When I look at pictures of the three of them dressed for church, in the bathtub together or playing with their toys now, I see a healthy happy trio. Though the day-to-day care was demanding, I tried not to complain. These were the 1950s when women were going to work and taking care of children at home, too. I thought I had it easy. One day when I was complaining about the housework Roy said,

"Ellie, we have division of labor in this household. I earn the money and you take care of the home."

I chaffed a bit as sometimes I felt that he had it better than I. Still I agreed and still do. If I were going to be privileged to stay home with our children then I would have to take care of the house too. Housewives weren't given much credit in those days when women began seeing careers as a viable alternative to being the supportive person for a husband. My being a housewife became a bit of a self-esteem issue.

I knew when we married that Roy's choice of profession would not provide us with a large salary. At the time that did not seem crucial. Money wasn't as important as love, and we had plenty of that. The first time that fact really struck me was when we began to look for a house we could afford to buy in Berkeley. It was my birthday when Roy called from his office.

"The Realtor showed me a house this morning that I think you will like and that we can afford. I want you to look at it. She can pick you up at noon."

When she showed me the house I cried. The Realtor looked surprised.

"Don't you like it," she said.

"This is my dream house? What is Roy thinking of? This tiny house, this cracker box!" I was angry. Like a child I wanted a bigger birthday present. Since it was the only house we could afford, however, we bought it, moved in and made it into a charming cozy home for our little family, living there happily until we outgrew it with the coming of our fourth child.

By the time Mark was weaned, life was slower paced. I was enjoying my body with its good health and vibrant energy. I had time for the family as well as the outside activities that I had gradually taken on. This period was of too brief duration. Just a few months after Mark had his first birthday I found that I was pregnant once more. This time I was unhappy. It was too soon for another child. Roy sympathized and helped all he could. Many nights we were both on our knees in the bathroom putting three children into diapers and pajamas. It was fun for Roy and he played with the children as he readied them for bed. I was tired after having the children all day.

"Just get them into their pajamas. I want them in bed, now!" I would snap. How would I ever manage another child, I wondered. Soon, however, I accepted the pregnancy, and it progressed normally. I took care of the family by curtailing other activities. I put my family first, my interests second. Wrapped up in my family I forgot my dreams of having another career. I had one already. When I was delivered of a second healthy boy, Paul, my joy was complete. Dreams of having six children no longer charmed me. Four was a perfect number.

When Paul was six weeks old, the other three children came down with chicken pox. With three sick children and a new baby, my energy was so depleted that I was unable to nurse Paul. I felt sad, cheated and guilty. The time I nursed each baby had always been such a special time. Paul would miss out. I cried for us both. He was our last child.

Roy did not share my strong feelings about having no more children. He teased me and made light of my concerns. I could understand why, and I resented it. He was enjoying success in his career while my career plans were fading into the background, farther and farther with each child I had to care for. He liked his father role, enjoying the few hours playtime he shared with them each evening after which we would put them to bed, and he would relax with me. The next day he was off to his interesting work while I was with the children again all day alone.

When my concern over getting pregnant affected our intimacy time he would say, "You wouldn't mind another baby if it were sweet as Paul, would you?"

"Even twice as sweet as Paul, I would mind!" I retorted. Though it was hard to convince Roy, I was finally able to get through to him that I did not want to cope with another child. He agreed that four would be just fine with him, too.

"Well, as a matter of fact, I am nearly forty. With Paul five now, it would be nice to get on with another life," he said.

Paul was like a family pet. Even though his older sister, Beth was only a little over four, she liked picking him up and carrying him around. I had to watch her so she would not drop him, as she was so small herself. Sometimes, to my dismay she would wake him from a nap so that she could play with him. I wonder how the affection we showered on the baby affected Mark, who was still a baby himself. Mark began to demand time and attention from both me and his father until his demands for attention became insatiable.

The other children learned about taking turns. Mark always wanted to be first. When we read stories together, Mark would push the other children away to sit beside me. When his father had the day off Mark would ask him to help him with a model airplane and keep him involved much of the morning. Later, when we began boating, he would want to have more turns on the water skis than everyone else. He seemed to demand so much of our energy that there wasn't much left over for us or for the other children.

As Mark grew he tackled projects beyond his capabilities, requiring involvement with either his father or me. When he could barely reach the handle of the lawn mower, he wanted to mow the lawn to surprise his father, whom he adored. We delighted in each child as he or she learned new skills, and we encouraged grown-up behavior. My favorite picture of Mark is when he was three years old. He is sitting next to his fire truck, which he has taken apart, his cap perched on his head at a tilt, squinting at the wheels trying to figure out how to put it back together. I had seen him out my kitchen window and ran for the camera in time to get a picture that is among my treasures today.

Though the children were normally competitive and fought with one another, my clearest memory is how easy it was for me to get my work done through the day as they played together. The four of them had their own playschool. During the morning I would work around the house while they played. I put all four of them down in the afternoon for a nap. When they woke we went to the park for an hour before dinner. While having them so close in age was difficult at times, since they shared the same routine, it was easier than having two age groups.

When it was time for our oldest, Beth, to go to school, she did not want to leave the others. For a number of mornings after she started school, she cried so much that her teacher brought her home early. When I asked Beth what was the matter with school she said she wanted to stay home and play with the others adding through her tears, "And bloody murder, when you get to first grade, I heard that they give you homework!"

It was hard to keep a straight face when I heard those words. Bloody murder! It was not an expression we used in our house. It was the beginning of a new awareness for me. The outside world had come in on our little family.

Mark started school in a mid-year class. In his second year, we moved from our small house to a large two-story house that would be our home for the rest of our children's lives with us. With the school change we decided to have Mark repeat a half-year so that he would be able to finish in the spring with the others. That did not pose an obvious problem and, in fact, may have given him an advantage.

In his early school years, he got into fights on the playground. He was frequently denied play privilege as he sat on the bench during recess. I worried about his ability to get along with the other children. When I spoke with the principal about my concern he said, "You have a lot in that boy. He'll be fine."

It was when he was about six that he suddenly began wetting his bed. We couldn't figure out why he should begin wetting at that time. What changed, I wondered, that he could no longer control his nighttime bed-wetting? If there had been another child, we could have made sense out of it. As it was, his brother, Paul, and he were both getting older and out of their baby needs (we thought). His younger brother had started school the year Mark was six. For a long time we were patient with Mark and tried to minimize the importance of this regression, confident that it would correct itself over time.

When it continued for years, we took him to a doctor who recommended a device that would ring and wake him up if he started to wet. Unfortunately, the bell would wake the other members of the family while Mark slept on. Once he was asleep it was almost impossible to wake him. I took him to a hypnotist when he was eight. When results were not forthcoming, Mark laughed when he told me, "When he told me to put up my little finger, I did. But I didn't feel any different before or after. It didn't work, mom." Another failure. I required that he change his own sheets when he wet. He did so without complaint. Still no results. Though it was disgusting to him, as he grew older, he was unable to control his bedwetting. It remained a problem until he was in high school. I derived some small comfort when I was told that bed-wetting was one of the reasons men were rejected for the military.

The children were all bright. They succeeded in school. Rarely did I have to help them with homework. I remember taking a course in the new math only to find that I couldn't learn it as fast as they. They didn't need me to help them. I had to ask them for help. When our second child, Deborah, was placed in the accelerated class, it was a disappointment when the next year Mark did not make the same class. We had expected he would and so had he. One of the teachers said, "Mark is one of those children who does not test well. We think he is capable of the work. Unfortunately, we place by test results."

I wonder if he would have been more challenged in an accelerated class, had more satisfaction and gained more self-confidence. He was an energetic child and never still. His older sister learned to swim. He wanted to learn. Not only learn but also be as competent as she was in the same time. He wanted to do the same things his older sisters did whether he was ready or not. His competitive spirit over-shadowed his judgment. He was not amenable to restraint or teaching. He was hard to hold back. One time on a family outing we were playing baseball. Beth and Deborah could hit the ball easily. When it came Mark's turn he could not hit the ball. He demanded that his father pitch him balls until he was exhausted and crying in frustration. He would not hear when his father explained that his coordination would develop over time and that he would learn as easily as the girls when he was older. He wanted to do it right then!

When the boys began to play out in the street our involvement with the older neighbors increased. There were complaints about broken shrubs, trespassing on their grass, small annoyances that made for tension. I pictured neighborhoods where families worked together on common concerns and would have appreciated more support from the neighbors to work out problems in a friendly fashion. We lived in a neighborhood where people wanted more to be left alone than to relate. One time a neighbor called the police because she had gotten frustrated with trying to keep the children from playing ball around her house. I told the policeman when he came to the door, "I wish she would come to me. I am sure we could settle our problems among ourselves." I was angry and frustrated, and I fumed that night when my husband came home.

"Where are the kids to play? They can't go down to the playground alone, yet. The city is no place for boys!"

"I'll talk to the kids. It sounds like you had a hard day. Mrs. S. does seem unreasonable but the boys have to learn to respect her rights."

I had grown up on a farm where acres, not houses, separated neighbors. I felt hemmed in with all these people to contend with. I tried to restrain the exuberant boys. I was comfortable with daughters. Anxious with boys. When they were out playing, I felt tense, always wondering when there would be a crisis.

Mark had a bad temper. It was some time until I realized how uncontrollable it was. When he was six I was getting him ready for bed. Something didn't suit him. He became furious, took his shoe and threw it through the window. That was the first episode that distressed us. It was frequently to be Mark that was the perpetrator of a fight or a problem.

One neighbor complained more than the others. She said to me one day, after he had talked back to her, "That boy is going to end up in jail!" I was shocked and angry and said nothing, seething inwardly I turned away. She seemed to have no heart. What made her pick on Mark like that? He seemed no different or more aggressive than some of the other boys as I watched them play. He was bright and had fine potential. He would not end up in jail. He was more open and direct, did not run away as the others did when there was something to be settled with the adults. Once the young neighbor boys threw an apple through my window by accident. When I confronted them they denied it until my husband told them he had seen them. Mark would not have done that.

I began to feel defensive for my son. I liked his openness, his bright spirit. I knew that if he was reprimanded too much and too unfairly he would lose his trust of adults. Maybe I became overprotective of him in my concern.

The children on the block called the complaining neighbor "the witch." Unlike the witch in the fairy-tale whose curse was later removed by the good fairy, this witch turned out to be right. There was no good fairy to intervene for Mark, and I didn't qualify.

While Mark challenged us constantly, our youngest child, Paul, seemed to grow naturally, easily, and caused us almost no concern. I began to favor Paul and scold Mark. When there was a problem between the boys I automatically assumed Mark was the cause. I reprimanded him so often that, looking back now, it seems the way he learned to get my attention was to misbehave. Consequently, he did not get much affirmation from me. He kept the atmosphere around in such a state of agitation that it was hard to feel affection for him at times except when he was absent or sleeping.

For the first four years of our marriage, I felt like we were on an unending honeymoon. There were the two years before the children were born and two years of basking in the joy of being parents. I felt as if I had married the perfect man. If he found fault in me, he was silent. He was kind, considerate and steady. Steady. Such an important trait. There was a man in my life that I could rely on. This was the most carefree I had ever felt.

After the children came, so soon one after the other, our responsibilities increased so fast that Roy and I began to lose sight of one another. Our precious time alone disappeared. The children occupied my time and energy, and Roy's professional life as a seminary faculty member and marriage and family counselor took him away from us sometimes for days when I would be left alone with four small children. When he was free on the weekend I had a hard time relaxing with him. I felt driven by all the responsibility. The children were healthy and energetic. With their many interests we were a busy noisy household. One time when I left for the store briefly I told Beth, "Keep the door locked and just be yourselves. If anyone comes to the door and hears the commotion, they'll turn and run." My way of saying that I needed some quiet peace of mind. I tried to rise before the children to have time alone and found that one of the children would invariably have the same idea and bask in some alone time with me.

When I recognized their hunger for special attention I set aside time for one child each day to do something special. How they looked forward to their special time with mommy. It was not easy to find the same kind of time for myself. I never seemed to catch up on the work around the house, the laundry and the shopping. One night when we returned from a vacation I dreamed that I was carrying in groceries which were piled in endless bags in the car, a commentary on the way I felt about keeping up on this family of six

I pushed at Roy to do things on the weekend. When I complained about my share of the work he replied, "Ellie, I work five days and some evenings, I'm not going to jump out of bed Saturday morning and get to work. There will always be work." I longed to get back to the academic world but found myself further and further from finding the time and energy to do so.

We had our share of fights with six different personalities in conflict at times. Later the children told us, "We had no illusions that marriage was going to be easy. We saw how hard you and dad worked at it."

There were many more good times than fights however. We bought a boat and taught the children to swim and water ski. We went on picnics on weekends, learning to leave the lawn that needed mowing. The children developed interest in art, dance and sports. There were music lessons at times. For many years beautiful Lake Tahoe was our favorite vacation spot where we hiked and water-skied with the family. We learned to take time for each other. When Roy and I went away by ourselves the children complained. However, one time when we returned Deborah said, "I don't like it when you leave us, but when you come home you're so much nicer that it is worth it."

Frequently on a rainy Saturday Mark would collar Roy as soon as he got up. He would engage him on a model airplane project or whatever his interest happened to be at the time. As he grew older, his projects became more complicated and took more and more of Roy's time. Paul gave up trying to get much attention from his father and so did the rest of us. While the children resented Mark for his demands upon their father, I was glad Mark was learning skills that would be useful to him and that he had a father who would spend time with him.

When the children were quite small and I was left alone to take care of them, I would find that by the time Roy returned I usually had a cold. I would then receive sympathy from Roy. I always thought it was because I was run down until one day I realized that I was unable to ask for Roy's attention for myself alone with four little ones clamoring for his attention. I was feeling neglected and unloved. When I learned to ask for time with Roy when I needed it, I no longer got colds to get attention.

When Mark began bed wetting and having what we then considered were normal growing problems, Roy and I thought that if we took care of ourselves and solved all our own problems, the children would grow naturally and healthily almost by guarantee. We took all the responsibility for any problems that occurred long after we should have held the children responsible for their own actions. Maybe we were overprotective, especially of Mark, since he had a harder time than the others in the world.

Sometimes I wondered if we were spoiling Mark when we gave in to his incessant demands. While he certainly was demanding, nevertheless we were proud of his brightness and his many interests. When he was working on something of his own he was full of enthusiasm and positive excitement He asked me one time to take him to the lumber yard to buy some wood for one of his boat projects. He was talking about what he was going to do. Then he said, "Mom, I've got another idea for something bigger when I finish with this boat. This is nothing to what I plan next time. I wonder if dad still has the plans for the boat he built when you lived in Wisconsin."

Mark was talking about a fifteen-foot inboard motorboat. I was a bit more alarmed than impressed. I could imagine the kind of involvement that would be required of the family if he were to take on another project.

He generally managed to accomplish things to which he set his mind. When he bragged about how bright he was I said, "Yes, you are bright and quick but unless you use your gifts for more than your own interests they will not bring you happiness."

He was too young to grasp the implications of my warning. At that time I did not know that children cannot think in abstract terms much before twelve. Mark was so bright that I would not have entertained the notion that he would not understand the connection between giving of self, sharing and happiness.

He was a persistent thumb sucker. All our efforts to break him of the habit failed. Consequently his teeth grew in crooked. He needed braces and it was an extra expense, which we could barely afford. I was frustrated with his thumb sucking and nagged him.

If there were problems with the neighbors around the children, we could be fairly sure they would be focused on Mark. He seemed to gravitate toward negative energy. As I watched I wondered and worried. Knowledgeable in the field of psychology, we were familiar with the theory of the "identified patient." That is where families focus all the negative energy generated in the relationships on one member of the family thus making that member the scapegoat. We did what we could to avoid the problem.

When I took a course in parent effectiveness I used all the communication skills on the children. Sometimes they worked, other times the children saw them as contrived and as ways to manipulate them and they resisted. I never gave up. I went to workshop after workshop to learn better how to be a good parent and to learn how to cope effectively with our life problems. I had lived in an atmosphere of sickness as a child and wanted, more than anything, to have health and wholeness around me; to be healthy and whole myself.

Chapter III.

It was a Saturday morning and Roy and I were lying in bed. I was about to get up when he spoke, "I had this dream. I don't know what to make of it. I dreamed that Mark was crippled."

"That's strange," I said. "He's about as healthy as any ten-year old boy I know."

"I wonder what it means?" Roy went on. I forgot for the moment that I had planned to get up and make pancakes for the children. When he rolled over and looked thoughtfully at me, he had my attention. I had always been intrigued by dreams since my mother used to tell me hers when I was a child. We lay there in bed and discussed his dream. We had recently become interested in analyzing our dreams to uncover their hidden meanings. Though we were not yet very experienced at doing this, we knew that sometimes dream figures were said to represent oneself. Maybe this dream was saying something about Roy's problems, about how he was crippled in some way. Perhaps a younger part of Roy was crippled emotionally from the time when he was ten.

"Somehow I think this really does have something to do with Mark," he said. "How can that be?" I added, mentally dismissing his theory in favor of mine, and got out of bed. No, I thought, it must mean something about Roy, the meaning of which would be revealed with time and attention. Our four children were thoroughly healthy. I determined that this dream was not about our son.

By the time I got up, the children were already fixing their own breakfast. I watched Mark pouring himself a huge bowl of cereal. He had forgotten all about pancakes. He radiated energy and good health. He looked so good I wanted to hug him.

As I turned my thoughts to the coming day, a nagging thought slipped into my brain. "Maybe there is something wrong with him". At the same moment a shroud of gloom enveloped me as if it had settled into my soul, and the mood would not be shaken all day. Suddenly overcome with dense depression, I fought the urge to retreat to my bed and cover up my head as I had seen my father do many times.

I refused to accept that I had a child with a disability, and certainly not one that we couldn't correct. Anyhow, I told myself, we didn't know that much about dreams. We were undoubtedly making too much of it.

If there were anyone in the family disabled, it was I. If there were some lack in Mark, it was due to my inadequacy as a parent. I picked on him too much. It was I who was depressed and in need of help. It was I who feared for my mental health, feeling sometimes that I was only a step ahead of falling apart. Though I managed fairly well to stay on top of it, I had been stalked by depression most of my life. I did not want to think about how depressed I had been the year I dropped out of college because I needed to earn more money. Then I began to recall a series of episodes that led to mounting depression and crisis. The same year I left college, I had fallen in love with a law student and hoped to marry him when we had finished college. When he decided to return to his former sweetheart, he told me in such a kind and loving way that I as unable to be angry or realize how rejected I felt. I did not even recognize the hurt and grief over the loss until much later, when everything fell apart.

When I returned to college in the fall with only enough money for tuition, I decided to work for my room and board with a family I had known for some time. I was there less than a month when I began to understand something that I had not seen when I knew the family only socially. The man of the house was like my father. He stayed in bed in the morning and did not go to work. He refused to take responsibility for the care of his family, his wife and four boys. I wonder what prompted them to take me in. They could barely manage to take care of themselves.

Sometimes there was no food in the house. We had to manage the best we could without him. He was depressed and unable to function. When he did work at something, it was impractical, like an invention that did nothing to generate income.

I have no idea how they managed to survive all the years I had known them. His wife did not hold an outside job, although the boys had paper routes and brought in some money that way. I did some childcare. Mrs. P would sometimes borrow the small amount I earned and never pay me back. I saw her dilemma and quietly seethed. I cared about the family and felt helpless to help them.

In that environment I too became depressed. Needing a secure structure at this time in my life when I was alone, I had hoped to find it in this family. Instead I found that I had fallen into the midst of an unstructured, insecure household. I eventually became so anxious about my future and felt so desperate that one day I swallowed a bottle of iodine, half hoping to end my life. It was an impulsive, unplanned act, and one I regretted instantly. When I did that foolish thing, I was less afraid to die than to live. In my despair and loneliness I felt inadequate to the challenge of functioning in the adult world. It was as if some sinister force was pulling me down into its vortex.

It was early afternoon. My sister, who was a student nurse, was sleeping in my room. She had come to spend her two days off with me. I was unable to tell her how depressed I felt because I was hardly aware myself of what was happening to me. I had learned early to pretend things were all right with me even when they weren't. As soon as I swallowed the iodine, I knew instantly that I had done a terrible thing. I ran into the bedroom and woke my sister.

"Sue, I've swallowed a bottle of iodine," I said as I stood by the bed like a helpless child hoping my older more wise sister cared enough and would know how to help me.

She jumped out of bed, grabbed my hand and pushed me in the direction of the bathroom. "Throw up! Right now! Do you hear? Throw up!" she ordered. I was so scared that I would have jumped off the roof if someone ordered me to do so and I thought it would save my life. When I stuck my finger down my throat the brown sticky liquid poured out. The deadly poison left my body quicker than it had been taken in. In a very short time I felt physically normal.

If anyone was frightened, horrified or angry with me, they did not voice their concerns in my presence. In my withdrawn, shaken state I did not hear what they said to one another. My sister told me to pack my things to go home to the farm. My host family never knew what had set off my violent reaction. Their family was as secretive about their father as we were in our home.

Once home, I withdrew so completely that for five months I refused to speak with anyone. I did not know what to say and felt sure that there was no help for me. I had no way to make sense out of what had happened or why I had done what I did. I was nineteen years old. Psychotherapy was not an option for me at that time because no one in our family had heard of psychotherapy, as we know it today. Because I did not know how or what to ask for I am sure my family felt helpless. I know they cared for me even though they let me be. For days and weeks I slept and ate and spoke to no one until finally, when I became thoroughly rested (for depression takes enormous energy), I began to read. I buried myself in books about people's lives, thus shutting out the nagging fears I had for myself and delaying getting on with my own. I read nearly every book I could find in the house, all the material that came in the mail and even went up to the attic to find more books. Though reading was a way for me to remain passive and unrelated to people, nevertheless it did draw me out of myself so that after many weeks, I began to feel like joining the living. Though I felt guilty for the burden it imposed upon my mother to care for me, I felt unable to care for myself. My father was absent. He was back in the mental hospital that winter.

It was a dreary snow-bound North Dakota winter. I lay in bed feeling as cold inside as the wind-driven drifts that accumulated outside the window. I stayed behind the closed doors of our family house from January to May. With the coming of spring, I recovered the motivation to get up and get on with my life.

I felt so ashamed of myself that it was years before I could speak of that time. Even now I feel that same shame in spite of all I know now about psychology. Since I did not talk about it, or understand what had happened, I continued to be an easy victim of depression for years until I was finally able to integrate those experiences through working with a Jungian therapist. Through the work and theories of Carl Jung, I was helped to make sense out of my experience and possibly was saved from a fate like my father's or Mark's.

When I began to understand that depression was a normal reaction to many of life's problems, that it was something to be experienced and not be repressed, I learned to face depression with less fear. I began to realize how much my life was influenced by my fear of being like my father. Gradually, through therapy, I learned to trust my own inner strength and my own capacity for health. By the time Mark was ten, I had significantly altered my way of viewing life. I was able to deal with daily problems and my mood swings in a variety of ways.

Raising four small children was sometimes overwhelming for both Roy and me, and we were regularly attending workshops and retreats to help us develop parenting skills, as well as resolve our own early childhood problems and our adult problems with each other. We honed our skills as counselors as we worked on our own lives.

When I was attending a seminar given by a Jungian therapist, she said, "Children are forced to live out the unconscious lives of their parents. If the parents fail to work out their family problems with their parents, their children are stuck with the problems of the parent."

This caused me to wonder about my father, who had been an orphan. At the same time, her remark inspired me to work very hard since I did not want to burden my children with tasks that were mine to complete.

One time a psychiatrist friend of ours commented, "I've never seen any couple work so much on their marriage as you and Roy." I felt it as a criticism until later I realized he was wrong about our focus. It was not only the marriage. I was working on my life. I was strongly drawn toward death, away from life when I was subject to depression, and I was compelled to build up positive experiences to offset the negative pull towards giving up on life.

As a child I had lived in an atmosphere of mystery with my father moving in and out of our home. I had, however, seen how little enjoyment he derived from living. Making my marriage as good as I could was only part of my work on myself. More important was my need to find my own ground, to anchor myself in the positive so that I should be able to face life with the same courage I saw my mother demonstrate as I grew up and later when she faced tragedies with her own children.

I turned to prayer and meditation. I took time to reflect and center myself ready for each day's demands, learning to take life a day at a time as we are instructed to do through scriptures. It was hard. I had a natural tendency to worry. In the catechism there is a commandment, "Thou shalt not conjure." I wished I were better at obeying that commandment. I often conjured for myself a fate like my father's. I turned to God. Though I rejected the traditional fundamentalist Christianity in which I had been reared, the teachings of Jesus drew me like a magnet. As I studied them, I saw in them the power for the healing I longed for and needed.

At the time of Roy's dream I had just returned from a summer seminar on the Records of the Life of Jesus held by the Guild for Psychological Studies. During those two weeks in the mountains, I had been thinking about our son, Mark, and how much like me he was. I was concerned about him even before Roy told me his dream, which I now so strongly denied had anything to do with Mark.

That night when we were alone, I told Roy how depressed I had been feeling.

"Maybe you're right about Mark. I think we ought to find him a therapist, don't you?" I asked.

"Ellie, I didn't want to tell you before because I didn't want to worry you, but I had dreams about something being wrong with Mark even when we lived in our other house, when he was small. I do think that we would be wise to get him some help. There is something that isn't quite right with him."

I felt relieved for the first time in weeks. At that time, I had complete trust and faith in the psychotherapeutic process. It had worked for me. I was sure it would work for Mark.

It was true, there was something different about Mark. It is hard to pin down because most of his behavior seemed pretty normal growing boy behavior. As I look back now I can see that there was less awareness of others and more resistance to socialization than in the other children. He seemed to need more attention, too. The other three children showed consideration to one another and to us. I don't think Mark loved any of us less but that he was so wrapped up in himself, his needs and what he was doing that he was oblivious to our feelings.

With such a large family, I always spent hours preparing dinners. The table would be nicely set, often with flowers. When we sat down to our meal any expectation that we would have a relaxing time discussing interesting subjects never materialized. If there were a few minutes of quiet Mark would kick his brother under the table, throw his peas at his sister or yell at someone for taking more than his share. He seemed to thrive on action and conflict. We often sent him away from the table to eat at the counter alone. Our isolating Mark did away with the problem of his disruptive presence while it created guilt in me for focusing negative attention on Mark.

When he would go out to play I would tell him what time to be in for dinner. He would sometimes fail to show up and we would either have to go look for him or eat without him. If he arrived on his own, he would burst into the room excited about what he had seen or done and want to tell us about it.

"You should have seen the big lizard Leslie and I saw down at the quarry," he would say as he grabbed for food with dirty hands almost before he sat down, unaware that he had broken into our conversation and that we had been worried about him.

Roy and I did not think Mark's behavior was seriously out of line and were often annoyed and felt pressured when the other children complained and demanded that we make Mark more accountable for his behavior. A familiar refrain was: You should punish Mark because he delayed our dinner, didn't do the dishes on his turn, and on and on. I would feel torn between letting Mark develop in his own free manner and correcting him too much. It was hard being a parent to four so different personalities.

In those early years Roy did not take Mark's behavior problems as seriously as I did and so we had disagreements over disciplining him. I resented Roy's passivity regarding discipline. He thought me too demanding. We fought over how to handle Mark. He learned how to set us against one another. He came between us. We became expert at a game Eric Berne, the transactional analysis psychiatrist, called, "let's you and him fight."

Mark would do something mean to one of the children, and I would yell at him.

Roy would say it isn't that important. He might say, "She probably asked for it." We would argue and Mark would walk away as if nothing had happened. Soon Mark learned what behavior bothered me and what Roy did not consider important and would do the thing that would set us against each other. We soon saw what was happening and agreed to work together to avoid the pitfall of making Mark responsible for our fighting.

There were complaints from neighbors, many of them I considered minor, mothers overprotective of children who could take care of themselves if their mothers would let them work out things between them. While it was unpleasant to have police at the door on a few occasions over minor complaints from neighbors, it was not until Mark began wetting his bed at six years after being dry for years that we thought something ought to be done.

When we finally took him for therapy I was advised to see someone at the same time so that the two therapists might confer with one another about our situation. This was a time when we all believed that if children had problems their mothers were at fault. I was glad to comply if it would help our family to get along better so that we could all be happier.

Together we went to our sessions each week. I enjoyed having time with Mark alone. He was a pleasant ten-year old to be with when he was by himself. With four children, sometimes it was hard to focus on one of them at any given time. These were special times for us both and Mark was happy when I picked him up at school to take him to our appointment. When our other children teased him about having to see a head doctor, I scolded them for their insensitivity. I told them that they would not have teased him if he had been going to the regular family doctor. I reacted strongly to that attitude toward emotional problems, all the more because I had felt ashamed all my life of my father's emotional illness. I did not want Mark to feel ashamed for needing help with emotional problems.

I recognized the same disrespect for the person with emotional problems I had felt as a child. The stigma was not only in the world. It was in me. Our children learned early and subtly how to stigmatize those suffering from mental illness. It struck me head-on when I wrote an article on Mark's illness for publication. The editor asked me if I wanted to use a pen name.

"To protect Mark," he said. Unhesitatingly, I agreed to a pen name. Later I thought it over. I was ashamed of my cowardly attitude. I called the editor.

"I want to use my own name. What does my hiding do but perpetuate the stigma around this illness? What am I protecting Mark from?"

It is only after years of furtive secretive living around this family issue that I have come out and am willing to own the story around my own family, to assume responsibility that is mine, to claim it all.

One day I said to Mark, "What did you talk about today?" He smiled, "I'm not going to tell you." I drove on in silence then he spoke again. "Mom, he wants me to bring in my turtle and my fire truck to show him next time we come in." I did not mind a bit that he was secretive. What gave me pleasure and immense relief was the lighter happier relaxed feeling that Mark seemed to have after each therapy session. It looked as if we were getting somewhere.

For a number of months we attended our sessions regularly while things went well at school and home. Tensions were eased but Mark's bed-wetting continued. When we were talking about finishing therapy for the summer I asked him, "Have you talked about the bedwetting yet?" "Not yet," he said. He never did bring up the subject nor did his therapist. He continued his bedwetting until he was in high school, when, for no reason we could figure out, he stopped. He was fourteen. Because other things were going well, in the fall we did not return to therapy. Later when we again attempted some family therapy, hoping to help Mark as well as ease the family stress, Mark was resistant. We did not succeed in all seeing someone together for our whole family more than a few times. One of the regrets Roy and I have is that we were not more persistent in requiring the children to cooperate.

While we had tensions and stress over the years, I did not think that our problems were more than average. Everyone seemed to have troubles, sometimes much more serious than ours. If I had known then, when things were going so well, that I would be facing the breakup of my family in the way it later came, I am not sure if I would have had the courage to go on as I did.

Chapter IV.

Family affairs dominated our lives. The children did well in school and learned many other things outside of school. The girls and I sewed together. Mark learned to play the trumpet. Beth studied and became a fine artist. Deborah learned to play the piano and Paul's budding interest in electronics blossomed with the encouragement he received from both his father, who had studied to be an engineer and his grandfather who was an electrical contractor. They all learned to swim and water ski.

By high school, Mark became a fine athlete. Beth joined the swim team at school. Deborah was busy with other projects for her accelerated class. One year we helped her build an incubator where she succeeded in hatching one duck. We took turns filling the jar with warm water to make an incubator for the pet. In the absence of a mother duck, the duckling adopted us for parents. When it was left alone in a room it squawked until we either brought it with us or returned to it. One day, when the children were in school, I went out on the patio to read. When the duck squawked in the house alone, I brought it out and put it under my chair where it lay content in the shade. As I got up later to go into the house, I spied a cat walking out of the yard. The duck was gone. That was one time it should have squawked and didn't. Deborah scolded me and cried when I told her what had happened.

"There isn't even a body to bury," she lamented. We all missed that little duck for some time.

We bought a boat. For many years we spent a week each summer at beautiful Lake Tahoe through the generosity of friends who lent us a cabin. We all learned to water ski in a warm sheltered cove on Emerald Bay and Meeks Bay, where we spent our days picnicking and exploring. Sometimes we brought along a friend or two of the children. I relaxed as Mark and his friend, Leslie, explored the woods and creeks in this limitless space of the Sierras. Tensions drained away as we enjoyed our time together. When we returned home, we were rested and ready to take on our routine schedules once more. All the rest of that summer we went to the nearby delta with our boat on the weekends. Life was idyllic for some time.

Paul was ten, Mark eleven the summer of 1966 when we painted the house. The six of us worked on our high three-story house from Memorial Day in May to Labor Day in September when the children returned to school. We had such fun as we climbed ladders and carried pails of paint around a house that seemed to grow larger the longer we worked. Paul was the lightest and took pride in working from ladders and painting hard to reach places. Mark was proud to display his muscle as he moved ladders for me as I worked in Roy's absence during the workweek. I remember Beth and Deborah working with us uncomplainingly all summer.

It would have been finished sooner if we had worked steadily. Instead, when good weather beckoned on a weekend, we put up our paintbrushes and went off with our boat to the delta to swim, play and water-ski. It was a summer balanced with work and play, the most cooperative effort we had ever made. We were all proud when we viewed our family project at the end of the summer. All the children learned to prepare and paint a house. That was the best summer we had during their growing years, as we kept busy together with a task that was important to us all.

That same year, still enjoying the benefits of work while he had money to spend from helping paint the house, Mark decided he wanted a paper route. At his age that was his only option for paid work. For a few weeks, in the excitement and novelty of the new job, he delivered his papers faithfully each morning. When this wore off, he began oversleeping, making his deliveries later and later. Our phone began ringing before seven in the morning with irate customers asking for their newspapers. I took on the task of waking Mark and getting him up at five. It began to look as if it was my paper route as I got him up and drove him some mornings. He woke others in the household with his fussing. None of us liked his having this paper route but since we thought it was good training and experience, we suffered through it with him. When it was time for him to collect people's money, he put it off until his supervisor began complaining. One day I asked him what the trouble was.

"I'm scared to collect from those strange people," he said.

I was surprised. He was an aggressively boisterous boy, reckless and daring, and I would not have thought he was afraid of anything.

"I'm not going to help him collect," I told my husband. "That is entirely too humiliating. It is enough that I have to get him up and drive him on rainy mornings."

"I'll help him collect," Roy said.

After Mark got to know his customers, he was able to make his collections.

He worked at his paper route until he accomplished his goal, which was to earn enough money to build a boat. He earned $1,000.00, enough money to buy materials for three boats, which he later went on to build. We were proud of his enterprising nature and his ambition, which knew no bounds when it came to projects in which he was interested.

I was relieved to be free of the early morning paper route. Therefore, when Paul shortly wanted to take over Mark's route after he quit, I urged him to take an evening route even though I believed that he would have done well in the morning. He was good about getting up for school. It was easy for him to wake by himself.

When he was not yet thirteen, Mark built his first boat. Roy's interest in boats was rekindled by this project. When he was a boy, Roy had built boats; his first had been a hydroplane. Together he and Mark designed a hydroplane similar to Roy's first boat. They sketched out a plan for an eight-foot piece of marine plywood. With advice from Roy, Mark went on to build the little hydroplane. He bought a small second-hand motor and enjoyed using that speedboat for a year after which he sold it. With the money from that he went on to build a sixteen-foot wooden kayak. The plan, which he found in a Popular Mechanics Magazine, had a removable mast so that the kayak could be used as either a canoe or a sailboat. Mark learned about fiberglass processing, as he had to make a deck, which was smoothly fiberglassed. Mark and Paul enjoyed the boat for a year or two after which Mark sold the kayak to Paul and went on to build his third boat – all this before he was sixteen.

His third boat was an even greater challenge. With the experience of building two boats before, Mark proceeded with confidence with the plans, which he had purchased. As I watched him work on his boat day after day, I saw the first signs of his compulsive nature. He sanded, re-sanded and worked the deck until the skin was worn off his hands. Nothing would do but to have that deck shining to perfection like a highly polished jewel. It looked as if he would never get the boat into the water. No sooner would he think he was finished than he would see a slight flaw in the varnish and he would resume sanding and finishing. When he finally satisfied himself that the boat really was finished, he asked permission to use our station wagon to take it to Lake Tahoe to try it out. Though he was underage for a driver's license he told us his friend, Tom, would drive. Equipped with a small outboard motor, the boat on a trailer and their sleeping gear, they took off early one morning. We proudly waved them good-bye and wished them well.

It had been a trying summer with Mark monopolizing Roy's time, taking over the garage and driveway and generally demanding attention for his needs. Neighbors had come to watch his progress and to compliment him. We were both proud and annoyed at how much family time and space he had been taking from the rest of us. Beth commented one morning in her frustration, "Mark, Mark, everything is for Mark," she fumed.

She had been promised the car for the day when her father told her that he had to take Mark to get some gear for his boat. She resented having to change her plans to accommodate her brother. It happened too often.

As we five sat down to dinner, it was a relief to have the boat and Mark gone. We had hardly finished eating when the phone rang. Roy answered to hear Tommy's voice. "In jail! What happened?" we heard Roy say.

When he hung up the phone, Roy was fuming. "That kid! He has no sense! You know what happened? When they put the boat in the water, they failed to put in the life jackets in their eagerness to get the boat tested. Tommy drove off to park the car with the life jackets in it. While he was gone, a police officer checked the boat and ordered Mark to put in his life jackets. Smart aleck Mark decided he would give the boat a run until Tommy came with the jackets. The officer was watching him. Because he didn't comply, the officer took him to jail. They won't release him unless I come up since he is under age."

We were deeply disappointed to have this happen. Our relief had been short-lived, and now Mark had done this foolish thing. We talked it over, since it was a long drive up to the lake and Roy had to work the next day. However, we knew a family up there who might be willing to help. When Roy called the police back, he found he was able to have Mark released provided the boy would leave the lake and go straight home. We had a contrite son on our hands for a while after that.

What did you learn from that, Mark?" I asked him later.

"I learned that when a police officers says jump, I jump," he said and went on, "The reason they were so tough was that just that week two guys had drowned through carelessness."

"You see, they were only looking out for your safety, not trying to punish you. It certainly spoiled your fun, though, didn't it?" After all, he had worked all summer on his boat and we were sorry to have it end so badly for him. If he learned a valuable lesson, it would have been worth it since he was given to impulsive behavior that carried the seeds of disaster in it. However, shortly thereafter, Mark would come close to losing his life in his little boat.

After his disappointment over the experience, he wanted to try his boat in the bay where we lived. There was no one to go with him that day so he asked a girl down the street if she would like to go with him to try out his boat although he did not know her very well. Roy drove them down to the bay, and they went out on the water. He came home and awaited a phone call to pick the two young people up when they finished boating. We had no fears for Mark's safety as he had been driving the boat for two summers for our water-skiing and had always been careful.

Not long after Roy returned the phone rang. It was the girl saying that Mark was hurt. We rushed down to get them. We found Mark pale and shaken. He had decided to try to water-ski once they had found the boat was able to pull him and he had been pulled under the water by the rope when it caught round his leg. Because there was no one in the boat to watch him, and the girl was inexperienced, she didn't see him go under and she kept driving until he had nearly drowned. His leg had been badly cut by the rope, and the fright he suffered from that accident took the joy out of driving his boat as far as he was concerned. He never used it much after that.

The next years were filled with us taking our children back to visit our own childhood homes. We went to see the farm where I grew up in North Dakota and the home in Minneapolis where Roy spent his childhood. One summer Paul and Deborah went back to visit Roy's family. Mark was nearly fifteen and did not want to go. He was still wetting the bed and he felt too dependent on us. It worried me a little.

The others went off to camp and made visits independently of us but Mark did not.

When Mark was seventeen Roy and Paul went to Minnesota to go fishing with Roy's family. Mark chose to stay home with me. Quite honestly, I would have preferred him to go since his intense personality wore heavily on me.

That fall we had a taste of our next stage of separation. Beth asked if she could leave us to live with her grandfather in Minneapolis during her third year of high school. I was proud to see her assert her independence but I felt a loss at the same time. One afternoon, after we had agreed to let her go, I went to the basement to cry secretly as I sat on the steps. I did not want her to see me weeping for fear that she would think I was trying to hold her back. I wanted her to try her wings even as I dreaded our nest emptying.

All the time we were packing to send her off I felt heavy hearted. This would be our first family separation. We had been close for so long it was difficult to adjust to the realization that our family would not always be able to stay together.

By the time she had been away for three weeks, we had adjusted well to being a smaller group. We even enjoyed having time for three children now where there had been four. I did not miss the fighting there had been between Beth and her brother and the fierce competition among them all.

It was late fall when we had a phone call. It was Beth, feeling homesick.

She did not say that she wanted to come home but instead she asked her father, "Daddy, when you come back to Chicago for your conference in November, do you want me to come home with you?"

We had become so used to her being away that we were not chaffing for her to come home in the least. Of course, her father did bring her back, and she settled down to finish her last year in high school from which she graduated at the top of her class and then went off to college.

By this time, I had been completing work each quarter toward my college degree in psychology and human development.

"Maybe I'll finish when you do," I told Beth. It was not easy to go to class. The quarter that I had to leave for an early morning class, I would be anxious all day until I returned home. The boys did not leave for school until after I had gone, and I was uneasy about their fighting. I worried about Paul because Mark's temper sometimes resulted in his beating up Paul when there was no one around to intervene. While I did not want to overprotect Paul, I always felt a twinge of guilt that I left him to fend for himself while I pursued my own interests. I was unwilling to delay my educational plans now that the family was growing away from us, and more reluctant to stay home all day.

Sometimes I would complain to Roy about being tied down with the family responsibilities while he was free to pursue his degree program and further his career. I felt really frustrated by how long it was taking me to complete my degree work. Many of our friends and colleagues were working as professionals and were already in degree programs. In our circles there were not many women staying home full-time with their children, and my self-esteem suffered as I confessed that I was a housewife when asked, "What do you do?" It seemed as if there was no honor in being a housewife in the eyes of the world, although I never doubted the importance of my role in the home. Our children were bright, involved and healthy; our marriage was satisfying to both my husband and me, and I liked having the freedom to stay home while the children needed me. Roy, too, depended on me for support, as I did on him. He needed me, more than ever to keep things running smoothly at home. I told him I did not resent his involvement in his career though I wished I could see more progress in mine. I was comforted when he said, "Ellie, if we do our homework now and give the kids the kind of start they need, when they're grown soon, we'll really be free—not like so many whose kids keep coming back home. You are doing a really important job taking care of things for us here at home." His appreciation went a long way toward keeping me faithful to the task at hand.

In fact, I must confess I enjoyed being home with the family more than I would admit. It was wonderful having a whole family unit, four children, a father and a mother, especially as I had not felt secure in my family during my difficult growing up years. Many of our friends were divorcing, and I saw the pain that such breakups caused. Even though I expressed dissatisfaction at times and complained a lot, most of the time I felt I was lucky.

I learned to play tennis and continued my education at the same time that I took care of the family. Sometimes Roy and I suffered from lack of intimate time with one another, and when our fighting became unbearable, we would pack up and leave for the weekend, coming home refreshed and ready to resume our duties once more. We had four teen-agers. The activity level ran high for years. There were few quiet moments during those times.

In our early years, as parents, our roles are clearly defined. Our task is to keep the children safe and to provide for them and teach them. As they enter adolescence, there is the war between setting limits and letting go to allow children to make mistakes and experience their own independence. As super-responsible individuals, Roy and I would struggle with letting go without feeling guilty that we were relinquishing responsibility.

When Mark got a mini-bike when he was fourteen, he was not allowed to ride it except around our neighborhood or in the country when we were on vacation. True to form, Mark violated the rule. One afternoon the doorbell rang. When Deborah came to the kitchen to tell me, critically, "It's the police for Mark," I replied defensively, "Well, at least things never get dull around here."

Mark had been caught riding his mini-bike out on the main thorough-fare. We grounded him for a time and there were no more incidents with the mini-bike. Next it would be a motorcycle. When he was old enough to obtain a motorcycle driver's license at sixteen, he drove one for a time. One day when he was going somewhere I noticed he had no helmet.

"I'm just going to the library," he said.

"Put on your helmet," I ordered.

Shortly after he left I had a call. He had been in an accident. A woman had suddenly turned into his traffic lane hitting him and throwing him over the hood and wrecking the bike. When I took him to the hospital, he turned out to be fine even though he had not worn his helmet. He had escaped serious injury once more. He was lucky. However, after a year of sleepless nights whenever he was out on his motorcycle, I declared that he was not going to be allowed to live under our roof unless he did away with the motorcycle and got a car. He promised not to ride it. Again he broke his promise. I delivered my ultimatum again – move out or get rid of the bike. I thought I was reasonable since there had been other dangerous incidents that affected my decision. It was with relief that I saw him drive his first car and he had it for some time before he had an accident. In fact, his first accident was with my car.

It happened one day when Mark did not get up for school, pleading that he was sick. He lay around all day reading in his room. Since he attended classes regularly I thought it all right for him to stay home. That night, however, he was restless and asked to use my car to go to a movie. I refused. He went to his father who thought it would be all right for him to go if he felt better and had been in all day. Roy and I argued and I gave in and let Mark go. We had gone to bed when, around midnight, I heard furtive whispering downstairs. Always a light sleeper, I missed very little that went on in the house. I wished I could have slept through more of the insignificant things. I jumped out of bed while Roy went on sleeping. When I looked over the stair rail I saw that Mark was talking to his sister, Beth. My first feeling was that of relief that my son was safe. I ran downstairs. "What happened?" I asked. Beth looked disgusted.

"Mark ran your car into a brick wall," she said.

He didn't look hurt though he looked frightened, certainly less aggressive than he had been a few hours ago when he had asked permission to go to the movie.

"It's that damn little car," he said. "I lost control coming too fast down the road there where it curves. It didn't hold the road."

"Are you hurt?" I asked.

"Naw, I thought I was going to get it when I hit, but I was in my seat belt. I'm O.K. What shall we do about the car?"

"You better go tell your dad and ask him what to do," I said grimly.

I was too upset to go the scene of the accident. Roy and Mark drove off to see what to do with the car. When they returned Roy said, "It's totaled, Ellie. I'm going to have it towed to the junkyard." "Totaled?" I screamed. "You don't mean it! If it hit a wall isn't it fixable? I want to see it. I don't want to lose my car!" Now I was more than frightened, I was angry. Roy had given me the little red convertible less than three years ago. I was not ready to give it up yet.

I felt horror when I realized how close Mark had come to killing himself. In my journal I wrote, "Mark wrecked my car tonight. I am searching for my own inner strength to cope with this serious situation."

The panic I felt is conveyed in the following entry, "I want to rush to the Bible or some other wisdom literature. It is not in my experience to find the help I need within myself." Like Yeats, "I lie awake night after night and never get the answers right."

There were many times in the following years that I felt the same helpless panic, that I had nowhere to turn and that I did not have the strength in myself to cope. But cope I did. The skills I had learned during my years in therapy came to aid me in my darkest times. Following the accident I wrote after a few days, "I think it helped me to write and paint and be still." Roy and I did not blame each other as we might have done, though we both felt guilty as if we had caused the accident by our disagreement. We renewed our determination to support each other with the best solutions we could elicit between us. We would not have survived those years if we had not stuck together.

The red Corvair convertible was the first car that was really mine. Roy had come home one evening and said, "I have a surprise for you, Ellie."

The surprise was the car, which we had all enjoyed for the short time before it was wrecked. Our oldest child, Beth, had learned to drive it the year we got it.

In a short time Mark had three accidents, any of which could have killed him. In despair I said to a friend, "I'm at my wit's end. I don't know what to do anymore. Each time he has an accident I think that perhaps this will be the one that will make him realize what he is doing and learn from the experience. He never seems to learn, never! He is walking in his sleep. What on earth shall I do?"

"Wake him up!" she answered.

I was frustrated with her reply. She seemed to solve her problems with her children just that simply. Nothing seemed to be beyond her ability when it came to dealing with her children's problems. I wasn't so lucky because Mark was not easy to deal with.

I spoke to another friend. I told her what had been happening. She was an experienced social worker and she said, "It looks as if he's trying to kill himself."

"Kill himself!" After the initial shock I realized that she was probably right. From my own experience, I know that we are held in a fragile balance between our life forces and our pull toward death. I also know that much of our behavior is motivated by our unconscious wishes. If what she said was true, then what should I do, I wondered.

"Why don't you talk it over with him and make a contract with him to keep himself alive?" she suggested. "Say you contract with him for the next six months, then after that six months renew the contract, that way he will have to face the stark reality of his death wishes, even though it may not be in his conscious mind yet."

I was afraid to bring up the subject of suicide, as if talking about it would make it more real. Things settled down for a while, as was the case each time Mark had a close call. He became helpful, somber and thoughtful. I hoped by ignoring what had happened, it would go away and we could forget about it and put it behind us. For a while we were caught up in making plans for getting Beth into the college of her choice.

Though our finances did not allow for the children to attend college away from home, with some scholarship help, we found that we could afford to send her away for her first year in 1973. This separation was not difficult. She was happy to be going off on her own and we were proud of her abilities, confident that she would benefit from her education. Since she was too far away from home to come home before Thanksgiving, we did not see her again for a time. We had letters complaining about the tumultuous atmosphere on the campus. "It was so scary. We were studying in the library and had to evacuate because of a bomb threat. It is hard to study in such an atmosphere," she wrote. She liked her roommate and enjoyed her studies.

These were the years of campus unrest and riots. Beth was far from home and lonely. At Thanksgiving she told us she wanted to quit and come home. We urged her to finish out the quarter, and we would discuss it again on her Christmas vacation. We hoped that she would adjust and stay the year, since we enjoyed our smaller family, and it was time for her to become independent. Before the end of the quarter we got a call.

"Mom, you won't believe what happened. I had this dream. I dreamed that I was trapped in my dormitory. I broke out the window of my room. And you realize I am on the sixth floor."

"That was a scary dream," I said.

"You don't understand. I really did break the window in my room. I don't know what is the matter with me."

I assured her that she would be fine, she was suffering tension. We would talk at Christmas. When she came home at Christmas, it was clear that she did not want to return to the campus so far from home.

"But if you quit school, you have to either get a job or go to school at home," I said and she agreed. After she returned home, she assumed responsibility for herself. I no longer had a little girl. She had matured so that I had little concern about her from then on. She fought with her brother less, got a job and soon returned to college locally.

Shortly after Beth came home, Mark declared one day, "Mom, I've decided to become an intellectual. I'll be going to college soon."

"And if you were to be an intellectual, what would you have to do?" I asked.

"Well, I have to start reading more. I'm going to get some books from the library, read some of the classics. I haven't read anything in literature," he said.

I smiled. It was hard to envision this boy, who had so recently become a fine gymnast and was interested and involved in many other sports, settling down to serious reading.

"Don't laugh. I mean to do it," he told me.

While he did well in school in most of his subjects, he had not been interested in reading more than was required. He began to collect books at library sales and flea markets until the walls of his room were lined with books on shelves that he put up as far as the ceiling. He bought many of the collected works of Jung. He brought the same kind of concentration to his reading the summer he was seventeen that he had brought to his boat building. I did not complain. It was less worrisome having him in his room than out somewhere with his car.

One day he had been in his room for a number of hours when he burst into the kitchen where I was preparing dinner.

"Mom, do you think I have been unconsciously trying to commit suicide with my accidents?" he asked.

"Why do you ask?" I replied. While I appeared to be only normally interested, I felt immediate relief. Not only that the word had been spoken but also that it had come from Mark himself. This was the first hint that Mark had any awareness of himself. My hopes soared.

"Well, I've been reading about the unconscious in Jung and I was thinking about all my accidents…maybe there's a connection. Oh, I've been reading about Nietzsche, too. He went insane you know."

While I commented to Mark that he was doing some pretty heavy reading, I did not realize that what he was reading needed to be integrated. That could only happen with therapy or more maturity. At the time, I was proud of this bright son of ours and pleased that he was interested in one of my teachers, Carl Jung.

That fall life became even simpler. Deborah went off to college. She had earned a full scholarship to a nearby university. Though she was close enough to come home any time on a shuttle bus that came to the library in Berkeley, she did not come home until her birthday in October. That Thanksgiving, Roy and I went to Hawaii for a vacation, our first holiday so far away from our children. We felt they were old enough to leave on their own. They were disappointed but managed very well. The girls cooked their first turkey for the four of them. We were trying our wings, trusting our children more each year. They were worthy of our trust. They took good care of themselves and one another.

One day in his junior year Mark came home from school; he hung around me for a while and I wondered what he was wanting. Pretty soon he said, "Mom, there is this real pretty girl in school. I've liked her for a long time. Today I got the courage to ask her out. She looked at me like I was crazy or something and walked away. She acted like she was scared of me."

Though I felt a pang like the rejection he must have felt, I wanted to make him feel better. I looked at him. His hair was rumpled, his clothes clean but ordinary. He looked like a kid that was about to go looking for lizards more than a young man that a girl would find attractive for a date. He had taken little interest in his appearance to now and rarely combed his shaggy blonde hair.

"Look in the mirror," I said. "If she saw what I see, do you wonder she turned you down?" When he looked in the mirror we both laughed. I knew he was hurt and bewildered. I felt sorry for him. He was so brusque and unpolished that it was hard to imagine him with any social graces.

But, was it only his physical appearance? Was there something else that put off this girl? It was hard for me to put that incident out of my mind.

Mark was already sixteen and had shown little interest in girls other than to talk about them from time to time. He related well with his sister, Deborah, next in age to him. He admired her academic ability and liked to talk with her. Now, the first time he got up nerve to ask a girl for a date he had been turned down rudely. I hoped it would not crush him. I began to see how sensitive he was, despite the fact that he protected this side of himself very well. Others, who did not know him so well, did not think of Mark as sensitive. He was prone to cockiness.

With a car to support and a growing interest in girls, Mark found he needed more money than he could depend on from us. He applied for a summer job as a bus boy. As a kitchen helper at home he was a washout. He resisted emptying the dishwasher when it was his turn and got out of any household chore he could. He never learned to cook, would go hungry if food were not put on the table for him. Within three days, he had been fired from his first job. He pretended not to care.

Remembering how devastated I had been when I had been fired one time, I expressed my sympathy.

He said, "I don't care. They don't pay enough anyway. I can make more money working as a painter. I can do something more to my liking."

I was disappointed for a number of reasons. First, I thought Mark needed the discipline of a regular job, second it would get him out of the house for a number of hours during the day and last, but probably the most important, if he was working, he would not be getting into trouble. This was a boy who had shown a great capacity for creating crisis situations.

After his rejection by his high school classmate, Mark did not pursue relationships with girls again for a time. He became interested in gymnastics and applied himself to improving his skills in all his sports. He played basketball with neighborhood boys. The weekends when we weren't on the boat, he was with his friends on the basketball court.

During his last year of high school, he began talking about an English teacher.

He pursued her while she tried to discourage him. He would not give up. When he finished high school and started college, he contacted her "to talk over intellectual things," he said. She was twenty-seven and he was eighteen. From the beginning, this was a destructive relationship. Both were individuals with serious emotional problems, hers more long standing. When I met her I was shocked at the degree of disability I saw in her. One of the first times I saw her, she had come with Mark to the country to see me. All the time we walked on the beach she was sipping from a bottle of bourbon. Mark told me that when he first had met her she had been seriously involved in other drugs. Her most debilitating problem was depression.

Mark was drawn to her for her fine mind, her physical appearance and his desire to help her with her drug problem. "She was a mess when I first saw her but something about her got to me. I felt such closeness to her, like maybe I could help her with her problems."

Later when we talked about his relationship I said, "Mark, you have problems yourself that you need to look at. If you hang around someone more disturbed than you, you won't have to see your own needs or do something about yourself."

He laughed. "Maybe you're right, Mom."

At the same time he pursued his relationship with his teacher, he began a business of his own, working out of our home, which became more dominated by Mark than ever. In the summer he got painting jobs through placing an ad in the local paper. By the end of the summer he was hiring his brother to help him, and by the next summer there were four fellows working together. Mark had a talent for dealing with people, surprising as it was after his newspaper experience. He got the jobs and estimated them for customers while the others helped him do the work. His business grew so that by the time he was into college the second year, he hired more people and began to talk of buying a lot and building a house.

One day Mark came home and announced that he and his former English teacher were going to rent a house together. We tried to discourage him but felt relief to think of getting him out of the house. He was monopolizing our phone and crowding our space with his business and his life.

I took the station wagon and helped him move his things into the house he had rented. They were to finally move during the next week. Maybe this would work out. It didn't fit with my pictures of the way things ought to be, but then I couldn't know what Mark's destiny should be, nor could I change or control it if I tried. I hoped, with all my heart, that this move would be good for us all.

That weekend we took Paul and went away. Mark was home alone. The things I worried about when we left home never happened. I was learning to let go and relax about the children, trusting them to be responsible. Usually I was not disappointed.

When we returned late Sunday Mark was waiting for us. He behaved naturally as I began to unpack our things. The kitchen was as he usually left it when he was alone. There were jars of food on the table. All the dishes he had used for two days were on the table, sink and counters. He had tools strewn in the front hall. I scolded him for his messiness and asked him to help clear up. Then I saw that the table was badly damaged. I looked up at Mark. He ran for the door. I went for him. As I grabbed at him I saw that the windows in the door were different. Where there had been beveled glass there was plain glass and raw unpainted wood molding.

Though he was much bigger and stronger than I, he did not resist, as I demanded that he come in and sit down.

"Roy, come here this minute," I yelled. "Damn it! Every time we go away we have to come home to find you in trouble. What in the dickens did you do?" I demanded.

We sat Mark down and got his story. His friend had decided that she would not move in with Mark. In his disappointment and frustration he told us, he drank a bottle of wine and had broken out the windows in the door and smashed the top of the table. He was sorry and would fix the things he had broken.

Once more we had a contrite young man on our hands, even a frightened one.

He realized that he had been out of control. Though he would admit to that, he would not discuss it together with us. We talked about his needing some therapy.

While we wished he would move out, we were afraid he could not manage his life. I felt as trapped as ever. Would my son ever get out on his own?

Deborah finished college and came home to live for a year and to work before graduate school. That year went well for us all. Beth was away and the boys liked having their other sister back. Mark spent time talking with her, looking to her for approval and encouragement. He admired her for her bright mind and liked discussing philosophical problems. For her part, she felt annoyed with how much of the household was centered around him and his business. When we demanded that Mark put in his own phone, tensions were somewhat eased, although there were still workmen coming around to the house with trucks and cars coming and going. Mark's materials for his jobs began accumulating at an alarming rate. He had vats and containers with lumber and tools lined up along the side of the house. The basement began filling up with his materials. He bought obsessively from flea market sales.

Mark and his former English teacher (M) were constant companions. She called him and came by the house in distress needing him for support while he had more than he could handle in his own life.

One morning he came home from M's house. His expensive sport jacket, which we had given him for his high school graduation, was torn and his windshield broken. His face was scratched. "How can you go on like this, you two?" I asked. "What's going on, anyway?"

"She gets so damn mad and upset. I guess I asked for it," he said.

We talked about their relationship. Mark was more open than usual that morning. He wondered, too, if he ought to get out. However, it was not until a year later that they actually separated. They even spoke of marrying.

"How can you think of marrying? You have so much to do yet, you haven't finished college, you have not found your life's work, and you have a great many unresolved personal problems, Mark." We would always talk. I don't know how much he took in but he listened. He knew I cared.

When I opposed his idea of marriage he said, "But I love her."

"I understand that, Mark. And it is something pretty special to have someone you love as you do her. You said yourself, so many times, that she is a pretty sick woman. What draws you to that? Is it because you are so strong? Maybe you are overestimating how strong you are. Please take care of yourself, at least put this idea of marriage on hold."

His business grew. He became more involved in his business and less in school. When he asked me for his tuition money for college, I asked to see his grades from the last quarter. He would not produce them. I suspected that he was not going to classes. He kept himself so busy that there would have been no time for him to look within to gain insights about what he was doing. Night and day he worked or went out with M. Soon he was sleeping around three hours a night, often forgetting to eat meals.

"I can't take Mark living at home any longer," I said to Roy. I was beginning to feel like a wreck. I couldn't sleep at night listening for him. His activity made me so nervous, I threatened to move out if he didn't.

"I think it's time he moved out. I will support you in that," Roy said.

Roy was less stressed than I because he was gone much of the time. Later we realized that he didn't want to see what was going on. Maybe, like me, he thought that if he didn't see it, there would be nothing there. He had worked professionally with emotionally disturbed people his entire career. If anyone could recognize symptoms, surely he should have been able to do so. However, blindness affects us when it comes to our own children.

We gave Mark six months to move out. In that time we had helped him buy a house with two of his partners. He had a place to go but resisted moving. The night he was to move he did not come home for dinner, and it was quite late when he arrived home. Though I was tired and not at all up to helping him move, I was afraid if I gave in this once, we would have to start all over again. Roy and I firmly and aggressively helped him load his things into the station wagon and moved him into what would be his first and only home away from home. He was there a year.

After he had been gone a while he came to Roy and asked to borrow money to buy some land so he could learn to build a house. He wanted to go for a contractor's license. I felt that we should not give him more help at this point. We had already signed for a house. He was moving too fast.

"He needs to work and save his money, Roy. We're not helping him by giving him money for more projects." We argued.

"Well, he could learn some more new skills. I think we ought to do it." Roy said. Though I disagreed, Roy went ahead and financed a piece of land. We were becoming more entangled with Mark's affairs. While the others were moving away into independent lives, Mark was hanging unto us and we to him. I chaffed under the arrangement.

After he quit seeing his therapist I noticed an intensity and a driven quality in Mark. He came by the house often and I wondered when he was working, or if he was. When I questioned him he would say, "Oh, I have to go out to make a bid. The others are on the job." Because I did not want to worry, I half believed him and tried to put the nagging doubts from my mind.

For the first time in twenty-four years Roy and I were alone once more. We basked in the new privacy, the simpler life. As long as I could allay my fears for Mark, I was perfectly happy. When Roy came home at night and I had finished my studies, we could lock our door and spend uninterrupted time with each other as we had our first two years of marriage before the children. I was prepared for a whole new life, developing my career and renewing my relationship with Roy. We were surprised how little conflict we had between us when there were no children to argue over or tensions around decisions with the children. Paul had moved into the dormitory and then into his apartment and went on to finish college. He never moved back home again. Maybe he was glad to be out of the atmosphere that had permeated the home for so long. I could understand. I had felt the same way when I had broken away from the family problems of my childhood. I was pleased about his independence and relieved.

Mark moved out in the summer. By December that year he was coming by the house again more than I liked. Sometimes I would come home and find him at the piano. All our children had keys to the house. We had never had any reason to lock them out. They were all welcome. Mark would let himself in at any time.

"I've been playing the piano for four hours, Mom," He told me one day. I didn't know what to say. So often I would scold when later I would wish I had said something supportive. Under my scolding was a growing fear. What was happening to this young man? I thought I knew a great deal about psychology and had a lot of answers but, when it came to figuring out this son of ours, I was stumped. All I could do was hope that he would see himself needing help. I felt incapable of helping him and frustrated.

In my childhood my father was running away. When I was grown, I felt like running away when things got tough, and now my son was running faster and faster Away from what? I knew that one must be still to explore and one has to stop long enough to do some self-examination. No one achieves consciousness by moving all the time because consciousness isn't somewhere out there. It is within. Health and wholeness is found within. Running away into activity would only delay the growing and healing process for Mark.

Though he had moved out of the house, Mark's presence dominated us as if he were physically there still. We talked about him when he wasn't there. We worried together, Roy and I. Mark began calling Roy at the office, asking for advice, demanding help with a pressing problem. And Mark's problems seemed always to be pressing. Sometimes he would ask Roy for money he needed immediately for something important. When Roy was not able to talk to him, Mark would come bursting into his office, demanding to see Roy. Roy's secretary would say that Roy was with a client. Mark, who had always been respectful and appreciative of the work Roy did, would pound on the door and demand to see Roy immediately. His problems took precedence over everything else. His own life and problems had become all-consuming for him. He could not see that anyone else had needs nor could he understand when we tried to reason with him and ask him to behave differently. He would say, "I don't know what you're talking about. I called you first. If you won't answer your phone, I have to come to your office. I needed you right then. It couldn't wait."

Things were getting out of hand. We didn't know what to do about it, how to control this child that was going full speed ahead in our lives, knocking everything and everybody out of the way.

Eleanor in High School

Roy on Motorcycle

Eleanor in her Prom Dress

Eleanor the Bride

The Bride and Groom

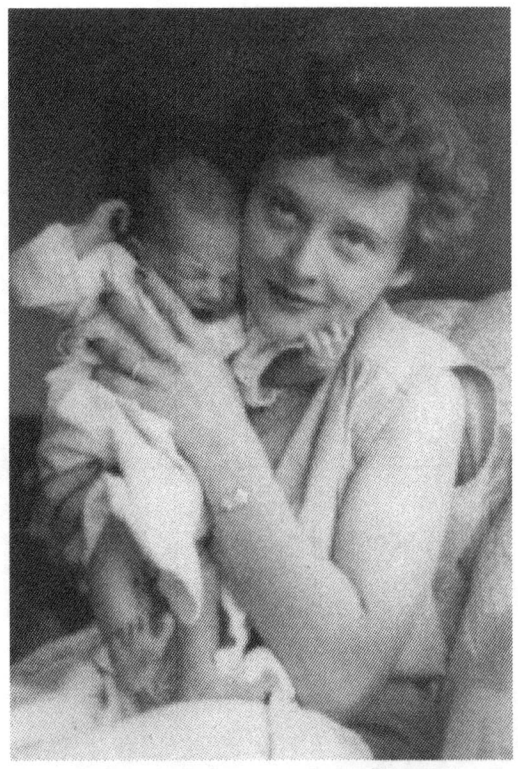

Eleanor with her First Born

Eleanor and Elizabeth

Eleanor, Mark, Elizabeth. Roy and Deborah

Mark in his Fire Truck

Relaxing with the Kids

Paul on Rocking Horse, Elizabeth Holding Deborah, and Mark

Mark as Mechanic,　　　　　*Paul, Elizabeth, Mark and Deborah*

Elizabeth, Deborah, Mark and Paul

Mark's Elementary School Picture

The Family: Paul, Roy, Deborah, Eleanor, Mark and Elizabeth

Family Portrait: Mark, Deborah, Elizabeth, Eleanor, Roy and Paul

Mark as a Young Man

Mark Builds a Boat

Roy as Chaplain

Eleanor and Roy

Mark, Grandpa Roy and Paul

Mark and Eleanor

Visiting Mark in the Hospital

Chapter V.

It was February 9, my fiftieth birthday. The day had been quiet until Roy came home and told me that Mark had been in the office and had made a humiliating scene again. He had wanted his father. Thinking Roy was in the side room with a client because his office door was open and empty, he hammered on the door until the counselor, who was with a client, came out. 'Where's my Dad?" he demanded in a loud voice. The counselor did not know and tried to quiet Mark who was visibly distraught. She later complained to Roy who felt helpless at being unable to control this difficult son.

I tried not to think about that scene as I started upstairs to dress for the dinner we had planned with four friends. Before I had finished dressing I heard Mark come in downstairs. He was loud and sounded upset and angry. I came downstairs to find him lying on the living room floor screaming, pounding his head on the floor and saying over and over, "I'm going down to Los Angeles to find Barbara Streisand!" Because he came to see us before he left, I often thought that he was hoping we would stop him. We tried.

We begged him not to go that night, to wait until morning to start driving.

We did not want him on the freeway. Roy suggested that we call a psychiatrist friend to get some medication to calm him down. He continued to rave, ignored our pleas and left.

By the time he left we were too upset to go out to dinner. I called and canceled our date, fixing a meal, which neither of us could eat. Before we finished, Mark's housemate came over. He told us that Mark had been acting violently for weeks and that he had just that morning smashed the wall in his room. He told us all that had been happening so that there was no doubt left in my mind that our son was, for lack of another word, crazy.

Though I must have fallen asleep sometime before ten, it seemed I had hardly slept when the phone rang. It was Mark pleading with us to come get him. "They're holding me at the hospital here. They won't let me go."

"What happened?" I asked. "Where are you?" I felt sick and frightened.

"Mom, I'm reborn. I drove off this cliff. I was going one hundred and fifteen miles an hour and I wasn't even hurt. I tore off my clothes and screamed for joy. I'm going to be all right. I'm born again. I feel like a newborn baby."

Because I had not had much experience with irrational thinking at that time, I hoped that this time he was right and had been born again and that he had come to his senses. How naive I was in those days, how little I knew. I went back to bed, relieved that Mark was in the hospital. At least he was alive and safe for the night.

We soon found that he did not stay in the hospital. When the nurses were busy somewhere else, he walked out of the hospital in his deranged frame of mind in Santa Barbara, where he crashed his car, three hundred miles away from home.

The next morning we had a call from a stranger. "Your son slept in my basement last night. He's acting strange and I would like him out of here. Would you please give him some instructions?"

The first feeling I had was appreciation for the kindness of this stranger who took in my son when he was in desperate need and could have been a danger. I wonder if I would have done as much for his son under the same circumstances. After I thanked him he let us talk to Mark. Roy told him to call us collect in an hour.

After we discussed the situation we decided that Mark would have to get himself home since he had gotten himself down there without our help. Though we weren't sure how he would do it, we had confidence that he would arrange something. Roy had an important meeting about his degree program to go to and I did not feel capable of driving alone nor of handling Mark. With feelings of ambivalence and guilt, we told him we would not come get him.

While it was difficult to say no to him, it was one of the easier times of the many to follow, when we would have to refuse to bail him out, rescue him or come to his aid. Though we suffered guilt each time we refused him, we did so in the hope that it was the best thing for him. We would have suffered less ourselves if we had helped him more.

One of his friends called to say that he was going down to pick up Mark. I made an appointment with a psychiatrist for Mark and me. When Mark arrived home he was distraught and extremely agitated. We tried to calm him down. I assured him that we would find some help for him. That did not comfort him. He did not want to go to a psychiatrist. "There's nothing wrong with me," he argued. I urged him to eat his breakfast and asked him to stay around the house. Unable to stay still, he paced the floor, opened and shut doors on the refrigerator, cupboards and round the house. He turned the TV on and off until I thought I would scream at him. I heard the front door slam and I went to look for him. He was gone.

When he did not return for our doctor's appointment, I went alone. I told the doctor what had happened, about my father's mental illness, how

Mark had been behaving and something about what kind of child he was. The doctor said, "Without seeing him, I wonder if he is a manic-depressive. It sounds like a classic case. My advice to you, as a doctor who sees people like your son every week, is to get him on SSI and let him go. He will rip you off for life if you involve yourself with him and his care." That was the first and soundest advice I would ever receive regarding Mark.

The doctor went on to tell me about a new treatment that had been effective with manic-depressives. "Lithium has been helping these people. You might want to look into it for your son," he said.

Armed with some hopeful news, I returned home to tell Roy what I had learned. He told me what had happened with Mark. "He's at the county hospital psychiatric ward. The police found him crouched on the sidewalk mumbling incoherently to himself. He told them he was counting the ants. They took him to the hospital."

Again we were relieved that Mark was in the hospital but our peace was not to last long. After a good night's rest, Mark presented a coherent picture of himself and was released. His condition had not changed, he was just a good actor. Besides, the hospital was so overcrowded that the staff was compelled to release patients if it appeared that there was a remote possibility that the person could manage.

For weeks we were overwhelmed with the day-to-day crises that occurred. Mark was on the run. He was unable to manage his business, refused to go for help and became more and more intrusive in the lives of all of those who knew him. He was running as fast as he could. I wished I could run away, too. I couldn't get away from myself or the situation. For days I wrote copiously in my journal to hold myself together. Sometimes I dreamed that Mark was well. The dream provided relief and balance to the stressful days. I felt helpless to do anything, to exercise control. I had watched my son running away from himself for a number of months. I said to him one time, "I think you are running away from depression, Mark. If you were to stay still to feel your feelings, you would find that you're not as high as you think you are." He looked at me and I saw tears in his eyes.

I had hit a vulnerable spot. I know we were all afraid to stop and take a good look, afraid of what we would see.

Though I felt the urge to run, I was determined to see this through. Early in Mark's breakdown I wrote in my journal. "Roy and I feel afraid. I feel able to handle whatever comes up. I feel strong. I am seeing my creation, and I will not run away. I will look closely and learn, learn, learn."

As a child I could not bear to look closely at what was happening with my father and even if I had I should not have been able to understand. I hoped that with our son, I should have the courage to stay involved and hopefully to see a different outcome than I saw with my father.

For a week Mark attempted to work at his business, but was unable to keep commitments to his customers and his anxiety increased until he became reckless and violent. We were unable to restrain him, and he was living with a friend who could not influence or help him. When the police saw him driving recklessly one day they picked him up because he became violent and acted crazily. They took him to the hospital once more where he was held for two weeks. When he was released he had no place to go. We felt he ought to be hospitalized longer. I spoke to the police about it.

"Until he does something serious, we have no authority to hold him," the officer told me.

"Serious—like kill someone?" I said.

"That's about it. It has to be more serious than anything he's done so far. He has to be a clear danger to himself and or others before he can be restrained in any way."

I was frantic with worry. It looked as if we would all have to stand by until this son of ours would commit some outrageous act before we could have him removed from the streets. What more would he have to do to demonstrate that he was a danger to himself and others? Every time the phone rang I expected to hear that something terrible had happened. I began to dream I heard a phone ringing. I would wake up drenched in sweat. Mark finally began talking crazily and hearing voices so there was no doubt that he was mentally ill, and the hospital kept him until we could make arrangements to have him placed somewhere for long-term care.

Our grieving began in earnest once the crisis was over. I cried so much I was ashamed of myself. When Roy would leave in the morning for work it would seem as if I couldn't go on through the day. When I was not crying I was walking about crying inside. We would make love. Unaware that I was sad, I was taken by surprise each time I had an orgasm when I would weep uncontrollably.

Though Roy appeared to have more control and be less affected, because he had to go to work every day he did not allow himself to feel as deeply as I. When the weekend came he would be so depressed that he could hardly do anything all day. While we knew the wisdom of expressing our feelings, it was imperative that we not be dominated by our feelings alone for we should not have been able to function in the world. It was necessary for us to get on with our lives even as we dealt with Mark's illness, which was threatening to swallow us both.

I continued my college courses. Roy stayed steadily in his job and worked on his Doctor of Ministry degree. Difficult though it was to stay focused, we were both grateful for the involvement that got us out of ourselves and our grief. While tears were a blessed relief, too many tears could drown us. Besides, we had three other children who looked to us for support.

Beth and Paul were around when Mark broke down. Deborah was away and thus from the beginning was not directly involved. We had been planning a trip to Denver for a professional conference and to spend some days with Deborah who was in graduate school there.

"I don't think I want to go, Roy," I told him when we began to make plans.

"I think you ought to reconsider," he urged me. "It would be good to get away and Deborah would be terribly disappointed if we didn't." We agreed to make the trip and hoped we could forget about Mark. Of course we couldn't put him out of our minds. We poured out our grief and worry to Deborah. She tried to be sympathetic but was in need of her parents herself and her resentment overshadowed her concern for us.

"I haven't seen you for months, and all you do is talk about Mark. I know it is tough for you but I am so sick of him. I'm sorry but I had so looked forward to our having some time together that would not be spoiled by something that Mark does."

We tried to be natural and act as if we were all there for her but there was no hiding how grieved and stressed we both felt. We still managed to have a good time as we went off for two days of skiing in the mountains. Even as we felt guilty that Mark's situation dominated our feelings and thinking, it was impossible to separate ourselves from him. It would be years before we came near accomplishing a separation.

While I would have liked more sympathy from Deborah, I could understand how she was feeling. She had needs, too. If I had any hurt over her lack of appreciation for what we were suffering, it vanished after we returned she wrote the following letter:

June 23, 1977

Dear Mom,

Got your letter today, Mom, and really grieved for you about the disappointment with Hayward. You could have used a boost, an upper, rather than the rejection on top of your other sadness. I admire your perseverance; I only wish the department had recognized how special you are and what a coup it would have been for them to get a woman of your experience and wisdom.

I wish you were here so I could give you the hug that I would like to give you. It made me sad to have you express your sense of failure not only with respect to academics but also as a parent. I understand where those feelings are coming from and that it is not possible to rationalize them away but I want so much for you to know what a strong parent model you were for me, how much I value you. Whenever I talk to Jim about my family I realize how much there is that I feel very good about and particularly how much I respect you and dad.

I can imagine how painful for the two of you this experience with Mark has been. As a sibling I have more distance and in addition I am so far away. But as parents, the impact of Mark's break must be devastating. It worries me when I think of the guilt or responsibility trip you must struggle with and I want to say no, no, no you can't take it on. That may be reasonable but I am sure it is not the way it feels.

I feel bad that I haven't kept in better contact with you. But the time that I devote to letter writing is all expended on Jim as well as are the long distance calls I am willing to invest in. In addition, I guess the distance from what is going on with Mark has been important to me and I have tried not to invest too much of my energy worrying about some things. Consequently I haven't sent so much energy your way as I would have liked. But my caring for the family is very much there, and I think of you often.

Take care. I will try to write more often this summer. I will bring Jim home at Christmas.

Love,

Deb

Over the next months and years the other children were involved off and on with Mark. Roy and I felt that, as our son, he was our problem not theirs, and we tried not to talk about Mark when we were with the family. There were so many times when his presence was a disrupting element and we had to deal with him that when he wasn't there we tried to go on as if he didn't exist.

It was not long after his breakdown that his mail began arriving at our home. We received phone calls from people asking for money owed them or asking when the jobs he had contracted for were going to be finished. There was a piece of land that Mark had bought with his father's help, hoping to build a house to help him earn his contractor's license. There were paint companies owed large sums of money. Creditors and customers called us and hardly a day went by that I did not have to handle some irate person. I didn't know what to tell them. Should I keep Mark's illness a secret so that when he did recover, he would not have to overcome the stigma that mental illness carries, or should I tell them what had happened? In the beginning we hoped that Mark would recover, resume his life and take responsibility for the mess that his business was in. When we realized that he would not be able to manage his business again, we consulted an attorney about how best to close out his business. We decided to assume his debts and sell off his property.

It was three years before this could be accomplished. All this time Mark's condition worsened. I was having to be cool and business-like with people who deserved to be heard but in reality I wanted to scream, "Leave me alone. My heart is breaking. I can't deal with you. I can't deal with your problems. Mine are enough." Even as I wanted to shut them out I heard other cries and one day I wrote in my journal, "This year is hard for me. Yet I feel related to the human race. Each day I hear of someone's situation more difficult than I could imagine bearing." It was good to stay involved. I felt affirmed in my good health, which held for years under constant stressful bombardment.

All my life I derived strength and guidance from the scriptures. I searched the scriptures day after day seeking to find, not only strength but also understanding.

If I could only make sense out of what had happened to us, I might have had an easier time accepting Mark's fate. As it was, I felt as if both

Roy and I had been diligent in our efforts to parent our children wisely, stayed home and taken care of them in their early years, had followed our inclinations to find help for Mark when we worried about him. Those were the things that were supposed to work to the benefit of children. In those days however, we were sure, along with other professionals, that Mark's illness was the result of faulty parenting. Where had we gone wrong?

Day by day I read the psalms asking for God's help, mercy, healing. I read the stories of Jesus healing the sick and casting our demons. When I read in Mark 9:29, "This kind can come forth by nothing, but by prayer and fasting," I decided to fast. I thought it significant that those words were written in the chapter by Mark the Evangelist. I tried to make meaning out of everything. In my journal I wrote, "Today I begin a period of fasting to pray for Mark's healing. I dedicate myself to prayer on his behalf. Jesus told his disciples that the kind of healing he did could only be done through prayer and fasting. I am not Jesus. I can only experiment. I am willing to deny myself and to pray for Mark. I have a debt to pay. I am willing to be used for the healing of others, namely my son, whom I have harmed." Later I wrote once again. "Mark's healing would have to cover a lifetime of illness. God is able to do above what we ask or think. I have doubts and will continue to pray."

When I told my sisters about Mark they began to pray and form prayer chains.

All the time I wanted to hope that our prayers would bring healing for Mark, in my heart I had doubts. I did not believe that the prayers were going to do anything to change things. I felt responsible for the prayer chains and guilty for my lack of faith. I was helped one day by something I read in Harold Kushner's book, *When Bad Things Happen to Good People...* "Prayer, when it is offered in the right way, redeems people from isolation. It assures them that they need not feel alone and abandoned...prayer is not primarily a matter of asking God to change things." I felt relieved when I realized that it would be all right to pray for Mark without asking for specific results. I came to a deeper, more expanded view of prayer than I had known.

At our church, when someone is ill or in need of support, their names are placed on the prayer list. My friend asked me time after time, as I resisted making public Mark's illness, "When are you going to put Mark on the prayer list?" Each time I would refuse to do it, I wondered if I was impeding his chance of recovery. Was I standing in the way? Maybe I did not want him to recover. Doubts ran rampant even as I offered up my prayers in behalf of Mark's healing.

The first weeks and months of Mark's illness, we kept hoping that someone would discover a treatment that would affect a cure. There were two things that were standing in the way. First, schizophrenia is not a disease that has a high cure rate and second, it seemed to me that Mark did not want to be well. We were hoping more desperately for his recovery than he. All the searching and effort to find him help came from us. Perhaps he had given up hope before we did.

During the six months that Mark was at the University hospital his mind was in a complete state of disintegration. He suffered constant delusions, raved at everyone and tried to harm himself so frequently that he was placed in restraints for days on end. Sometimes we would be told that we could not visit him. When we did visit he would refuse to talk to us and would vent his rage and fury at us. He blamed me for his situation for having a crazy grandfather. He always seemed to know us, and there was a thread of sanity running through his sadly deranged mind. He could tell us telephone numbers of his friends, remember things about the family and his other life, and he would sometimes ask about his friends.

We asked that Mark be treated for manic-depression with lithium when all the other treatments failed. The staff continued to refuse. When Deborah came home, reviewed the records and talked to the doctor about what she thought, since she had been training as a child psychologist in a hospital where she saw patients like Mark and knew her brother intimately, she too asked that they try lithium. They still refused to consider another diagnosis.

When Mark became more violent and ill I became impatient and angry with the staff. I felt that they hadn't done a thing for Mark to help him, and yet they resisted trying another treatment. They adamantly refused to consider that there might be some hereditary factor and that Mark's illness may not have been different from my father's. The problem was that there were complicating factors that made it difficult for them to make a clear diagnosis of manic-depression. The doctor said, "It is his delusional thinking and his violent outbursts that make it impossible for us to abandon the schizophrenia diagnosis.

Months after Mark had been given a variety of drugs that did not help him, he became seriously physically ill from the side effects. He was transferred to the medical unit of the hospital where we found him in a catatonic state when we came to visit.

I was shaken when I saw him. He was barely recognizable. When I touched him, his body was rigid as that of a statue. His eyes stared vacantly out of sunken cheeks and he was so thin he looked like a child. When I kissed him, he gave not the slightest sign of recognition. My effort to smile failed, and I ran out of the room and sobbed behind the door where a nurse found me and tried to comfort me. My father had never been like this, even at his worst. I felt shocked at the sight, and my hopes for our son plunged.

I thought I had finished all my crying but then when I got into my car to drive to class the next morning, I began crying so that I could hardly see. Taking the curve leading from the on-ramp to the freeway too fast, I hit the side of the hill and tore the trim from my car. Though I was considerably shaken, I was grateful that the accident was not more serious, and I continued on to class. The thought of going back to an empty house to cry alone was more frightening than braving the freeway.

One of the lecturers was a medical doctor. After class I spoke to him about Mark. When he saw how shaken and grieved I was, he said, "You have to find yourselves a support group. This is something you just can't go through alone." I thought about what he had said. I wondered if he would join a support group if it happened to his son. My husband and I did not want to seek out others with similar problems. Firstly, we were ashamed to tell others and secondly, we did not want to hear about other people's problems. Our own were sufficient. When one day an announcement of a support group for families of schizophrenics came to the house, I picked up the phone and called to inquire about it, pretending that I had only a professional interest. I was not ready to admit that I had any personal interest in such a group, even to a stranger. The woman answering the phone said, "Oh, yes, the group meets Tuesday at seven. I can't tell you much about it because I don't go myself." That was enough for me. I never, for years, gave another thought to joining a support group.

Roy continued working on his doctor's degree and I continued to attend classes and went to see Mark regularly. We were the only ones that visited. If he were ill with any other disease, I think some of his friends might have visited, but no one wanted to go near him in a psychiatric ward.

Dealing with our emotions, continuing our daily tasks and handling Mark's business problems were quite enough to take up any time and energy we had. Adding a support group would be another thing too many.

Returning from classes, it seemed I would just open the front door when the phone would ring. I would then be confronted with immediate problems to solve concerning Mark's business. Once his housemate called. "Mark has three old cars here. Would you take care of disposing of them?" Mark had a friend who fixed cars. Mark would buy old cars and have Jim fix them up, and then he would resell them. Roy arranged to have them brought to our house, one by one, where they sat until we could find someone to take them off our hands. My resentment began to grow again with all the problems we had to deal with day by day.

We advertised to sell the land that Mark had bought. We thought we had a buyer and were relieved, but when the deal fell through, I raved like a mad woman. I felt as if I could not bear one more thing. When I stood in line for Mark's SSI, I felt like a victim completely helpless and ashamed.

"Why should I have to do this at this time in my life? What have I done to deserve this?" I said, feeling sorry for myself. When I had a letter from my sister telling me she never felt sorry for herself or asked why when her daughter had cancer, I felt guilty about my feelings of resentment. Because I harbored resentment and guilt, I was not easy to live with and I felt sorry for Roy. His grief was as great as mine, and it wasn't fair for him to have to put up with such a negative woman.

When Mark was transferred to the medical unit, he was taken off all drugs. Only a few weeks after medications were withdrawn, to everyone's amazement he became lucid and completely recovered his mental stability. There was no reason to keep him in the hospital and there was nothing more to be done for him there. However, we did not think he was ready to work and he had no place to go after release. We arranged for him to go to a halfway house where he would be allowed to live for three weeks. We either went to see him daily or, now he was able to go out on his own, he would come to see us. The staff liked him and he got along well. He was worried about getting back to work, not knowing what reception he would receive from his former partners. Though we had not yet sold the house he had been living in, the partners were not willing for Mark to come back, and we did not think he should go back into that environment either. He seemed too fragile for ordinary living conditions. Even when he was well he did not do a good job of taking care of himself. We felt he would need further treatment.

We were not yet convinced that Mark should be treated as a schizophrenic, but we had no alternatives. Roy had attended a professional conference on schizophrenia and was impressed with one of the speakers, who told of a treatment center that he ran in Southern California. He said that the recovery rate there ran higher than normal—a nice selling point to interest people like us.

Roy came home that night, enthusiastic about what he had heard.

"Ellie, I think we ought to give it a shot if Mark will cooperate. Mark is not ready for the world and this would be a safe environment for him to get some therapy over the long term. He may be ready and open to working on himself now after what he has been through."

"Can we afford it?" I asked.

"We'll find the money. At least we can give it a try. Maybe there will be some money left from some of the assets when we get things settled over the business," Roy said.

There was no further question in my mind that this was the thing to do, maybe even an answer to our prayers. My hopes were high and it was only a matter of convincing Mark.

That evening we went to the halfway house. When we talked with the counselor, we were told that Mark would have to leave the next day, so there wasn't much time to decide what to do. We were all agitated as we sat down and talked. Roy told him about the center. "I'll take you down, Mark," Roy said. "It's a chance of a lifetime. You must go."

"I want to get a job. I want to work," Mark replied.

"What will you do? Where will you live? You have to be out of here tomorrow." He was pale and silent and looked so downcast that I cried inside. He was slumped in his chair dejectedly. His social worker was studying him. "You will have to decide, Mark. Your folks want to help you. There are no compromises. This is your last night here. We have to move you out to make room for others. This is not a residential facility."

Mark hardly looked up. He looked as if he didn't care what happened to him.

I prayed, "God, help us." Almost at the same instant Roy had a brilliant thought.

"Remember, Mark, one time when you went fishing with me at Jenner? We took out the boat and were going to go out the mouth of the river into the ocean. It was a rough ocean, the wind was blowing across the water. The waves were cresting at about fifteen feet for a while, exceedingly intimidating surf for our small boat. We counted the waves, waited and counted some more, waiting for a lull in the wave pattern. I was scared. 'I don't think we ought to go, Mark,' I said. We circled for a while as I prepared to give up and turn back. Suddenly the right moment came and you screamed, 'Go, go, go, Dad!' I went. We were out beyond the breakers in nothing flat. Remember the jubilation we both felt and how we yelled and laughed when we made it out in the smooth ocean and shared our fishing day? Remember that, Mark?"

A tiny smile appeared on Mark's face. Roy's story pulled him out of his passivity. Roy saw him respond and added, "Mark, now I am saying, go, go, go!" Praise God. Roy had reached him. He agreed to go. Within an hour, we collected some of his belongings. Roy and Mark went the next day to the center.

Though he was twenty-two, this was the first time that Mark had been away from home completely on his own. We were all anxious about the separation. Mark called us constantly, which kept us involved, and we asked the staff of the treatment center to keep us informed, I was afraid to trust the caretakers, sure that they needed input from me about Mark. They assured me that they would keep in contact but urged Roy and me to separate from Mark, to let go.

Letting go of healthy children is not easy. It is even more difficult with a child who is ill. It was a constant problem to know how much to stay involved and how much to let go. If I did not contact Mark for some time, I felt that I was being an unloving parent and worried that Mark would feel it as rejection, which would exacerbate his condition. I could not stop feeling responsible for him.

When Mark had been in the treatment center for a number of months I received the following letter, from his chief caretaker, a social worker.

"Well, the dam has burst for Mark, which means that he trusts us. All of his pain and anger and fear are coming out. At times he is wildly uncontrollable (these times occur when he is away from us at D-4). In his wildest ravings, we have been able to gain his trust and he is able to calm himself. He has been destructive to property at D-4 and twice they have threatened to have him vacated. This has been our main problem at this point. Should we have to move him, we shall surely let you know. We have also complied with your request for no medication, which makes the administrator rather nervous. I have spent many hours with Mark over the past five days and feel I have accomplished a tremendous amount with him. He has told me just about everything there is to say about himself and his problems. He also feels a real sense of hope for himself.

Yesterday Mark felt a great deal of terror over his lack of control. He is looking for a strong hand to help him and we are giving it to him. He responded very well to verbal direction to slow down. The biggest problem we are facing is the possibility that Mark will do something that will land him in trouble. We are watching closely and hope to avoid this. There is much cause for hope about Mark's future as we begin to integrate this material..."

My hopes soared when I read, "there is much hope for Mark's future." I hardly saw anything else in that letter. I wanted to shout for joy... "There is hope, there is hope!" I could sleep nights again knowing Mark was being cared for and that I should be able to look forward to having our son back home as a recovered schizophrenic.

Sadly, Mark did not last beyond five months in the center. One weekend he got out of control at the board and care home where he was living when he was not at sessions in the center. His treatment center was not called. The director of the home found it a convenient time to have Mark removed and called the police who took him to jail. By the time his social worker got to him, it was too late to have him back in the center. He was psychotic, so out of touch with reality that no one could reach him. When it was determined that he belonged in a hospital, not in jail, he was transferred to a private hospital where his condition was assessed as being beyond reasonable help. He was transferred to the local state hospital where he remained for eight months.

The daily stress and worry over what Mark would do next was removed. My thoughts were not as cooperative in letting things be. I thought about Mark night and day, dreamed about him when I was asleep. Nearly every journal entry I made has some reference to Mark or my feelings about his situation. March 6, "dreamed Mark well." Woke crying. March 18, "my daily prayer is that I shall be able to separate from Mark. It is so painful being attached as I am." March 22, "told Roy I am going to give up on Mark." April 21, "Sick to my stomach, Mark's business getting to me." April 24 "dreamed about Mark. Woke to a telephone ringing." When I woke there was no telephone. This was my reoccurring dream that Mark was calling for help. I would wake with a start and feel worried and despondent much of the day.

We visited with our other children, went on trips, went to our home at the mouth of the Russian River where we would walk along the beach hoping for healing for our woes. Nothing assuaged the pain and the longing for things to be as they had been. I longed to be free of the albatross of illness that clung to me. I had always thought of the ocean as a healing place but I found no healing for my pain. One morning I woke from a dream. I wrote in my journal, "I heard the voice of God saying, 'let it be. There is nothing to do.'" All that day I felt strangely light and comforted. Days like that kept me from sinking into an abyss from which I could not extricate myself. No matter how low I would be, there was always something that pulled me back into my own life reminding me that I was a person, separate from my son and that I owed it to myself and my children to affirm my life and my good health. It was my duty to be an example to them. Those thoughts kept me going over rough roads day by day. I refused to give in to depression, to let my feelings rule my life. I had a strong will. I aligned that will to a higher will. My prayer became focused. Daily I meditated, prayed and asked God for strength and guidance.

Because we were nearly five hundred miles from where Mark was hospitalized, we did not go to see him as regularly as we had when he was near home. It was some months since he had been gone when Roy had a conference situated near Mark. He arranged a visit. When he returned with Mark's personal possessions and reported on his condition, we cried together. I wrote in my journal, "Poor Mark. When I found the book *The Exorcist* in Mark's things, I almost could be persuaded to believe in demon possession. Mark seems demon-possessed. The way he is acting is not the way he acted growing up. Not all that rage, that destruction. Sometimes he was angry but not too far from normal. It is hard to focus, right now."

Deborah was getting married in August. It was a happy time for her. I wanted to be happy, too. With the planning for the wedding, I would forget about Mark for a day or two. The phone would ring in the middle of the night. Mark would be calling collect to "see if you are still alive. I dreamed I killed you," he said one night. He would go on with wild senseless talk until I would hold the phone away from my ear to shut it out. I didn't want to shut him out. I would calmly say, after he had made contact with me, "I want to go back to bed now. I am going to say good night." It was useless to reason with him or point out the outrageous hour that he had wakened me. He was too much in his own fantasy world to enter mine. My only hope and prayer was that if there was a sane side to him that he'd know I loved him. By now I was beginning to understand what a terrible place he was in and to have compassion for him. Sometimes I would be angry at the "wasted call." It would not seem that he derived anything from making it. Maybe he needed to make contact to remember that there was a time when he was part of our family. He was alone far from home. I could only guess what went on for him. His world and mine did not make contact.

Since Mark's illness had intruded upon many family celebrations the past months, none of us were sorry that he was not going to upset

Deborah's wedding. When she was finishing her dress the day before her wedding she said, "Mom, I'm really glad Mark's far from here this week."

I did not tell her what I felt but replied, "Me, too." Even the most joyful occasions in the future would always be slightly tinged with sadness. Since everyone is supposed to cry at weddings, I did not feel overly concerned that guests saw me crying at Deborah's wedding. They would think I was crying for joy. I felt no joy when I looked over the Berkeley hills out at the bay high above the city where we were holding the wedding in our beautiful outdoor seminary chapel and remembered when Beth was married earlier and Mark had arrived late for the wedding rehearsal. What fun we had that night and the following days. I was sad that Mark was missing this wonderful day of Deborah's. He had been so close to her when they were children.

Though I believe I managed to cover my negative feelings, I was angry with myself that I was obsessed with thoughts of Mark when he wasn't even near the place to cause any difficulty. Why couldn't I let go? Damn it, why did I always have to bring him into everything? Damn it, damn and damn again. It was Deborah's day and I kept bringing in her brother. I was smiling on the outside, saying all the right things to guests while I felt like the burden I carried was too heavy to bear and I had to keep it all inside. Many people there didn't know about our son and there was no one to talk with about all these feelings. I felt alone in the midst of the celebration.

Night after night I continued to dream about Mark. July 6, "Last two nights dreamed of Mark. I am holding him on my lap. Sure the doctor will criticize me and say that I made him sick. Have a phone call Mark says, 'da da' like a baby. Oh, Mark," I say. He says, 'I think I am getting better.' Another dream, Mark lying in bed, eyes closed. Roy beside him and I looking on. Mark wakened and began hugging his Dad. Doctors looking on. Mark very sound. He looked up at me and wanted to hug me. I lie down beside him and we hug and hold on. I crying and not let go. I know the doctors think I ought to let go."

I really wanted to let go. I felt bound by guilt, shame and grief. Though I wanted to believe that Mark's condition was hereditary, I still believed, as did many health professionals, that Roy and I were the cause of Mark's illness. We said to ourselves and each other all the things they never said. "You should have been harder on him, demanded more of him. You spoiled him. You let him get away with too much. You should have held him accountable for his bad behavior. There should have been consequences for his rebellious deeds," and on and on.

To add to the incriminating voices there were strange people and events that came into our lives. One day when the phone rang I picked it up to hear a woman's voice, "I heard what happened to your son. You deserve it, you bitch!" She then hung up. After the initial shock, I realized that it sounded like the voice of a woman I knew who was miserable because of the breakup of her marriage and her failing health. I had never done her any harm nor wished her ill. With that knowledge, thank God, I was able to let go of the hurt and shock very quickly. I remember screaming, "God, this is too much! Too damn much! What do You want of me?"

Chapter VI.

It had been months since I had seen Mark. I missed him. One morning I said to Roy, "Honey, do you think we could take a trip down to see Mark? I could arrange a few days if you can. Maybe we could make a short vacation of it."

"Ellie, I didn't want to tell you how bad he was when I saw him. He's probably not going to know you. I don't think you will like what you see. Are you sure you want to go?" Roy replied.

When I looked at him I felt his love and concern for me. "Maybe I won't like what I see but I think about Mark constantly anyhow and have all kinds of pictures of his situation. Maybe it would be easier if I saw how it really is, and then I wouldn't have to make up pictures. Yes, I want to go. It might be good for Mark to have us come. Don't you think he feels pretty deserted and alone?"

My husband looked thoughtful, "I don't know what he feels or thinks. He's pretty far-gone to read what his reactions are. It has been a long time since I saw him. I would like to go, too. I can get off next week."

I was prepared to be shocked and wasn't disappointed. A two-year old is more advanced than Mark was that day. He showed no signs of recognition as he paced the grounds, walking slowly back and forth, sometimes bumping into an object then examining the object and turning and walking in the opposite direction. He was mute. His eyes were vacant and staring, like a blind person. I took his arm and walked with him, hoping to make contact. There was no response. We did not have to stay long to know that there was nothing we could do for Mark. In a short time I had seen enough and asked to leave.

We agreed that we would not talk about Mark when we returned home but to try to forget about him unless there was something we could do. We refused to talk with our other children. We could not deal with their feelings and our own. We thought we were protecting them by hiding our grief.

Whether it was right or wrong, I had to take care of myself to survive those awful days and weeks. If I talked about Mark, I felt worse than if I contained those feelings and wrote in my journal and drew pictures of them. My journal is filled with drawings of the feelings of those days. In March I wrote, "Mark sent to C State Hospital. I am glad I can sleep again. April 4, a drawing, underneath written, "Give us this day…our deepest desires…our longing to be related to reality." I remained grounded as I worked through resentments, questions and answers in my journal. If I did my other children a disservice by sharing so little with them, it was only because I loved them and believed that they had enough in their own lives to handle and that dealing with their mother's feelings would burden them even more.

In the busy days that followed our return we had no communication with the hospital. We pursued the task of settling Mark's business. I took care of the daily mail and phone calls. Roy called and spoke to creditors assuring them that we would pay them as soon as we settled some of the problems related to the sale of land and house. While the bills that came were threatening in nature, when I called and spoke to individuals we were given consideration and kind treatment. While I felt harassed by the myriad problems arising from the complications of his business, I was grateful for every small kindness shown me.

In the beginning we had hoped that Mark might recover and resume his business and it was hard to know what to tell customers and creditors. As time went on, we decided to tell them that Mark was ill and might not return. It was years before we told where Mark was when he was in the hospital. As someone who is not only honest but also sometimes blunt, I had difficulty covering the truth. Roy, who is a careful tactful person, found it less difficult.

While I resented the responsibility of settling Mark's business, there was the redeeming factor that it was something positive that we could do. There was the possibility of recovering some of the money we had invested as well as paying for Mark's care if there was money left over. It was another practical task that served to ground us both. When we would want to dissolve in tears, we would have to deal with an immediate problem that would keep us from dwelling on ourselves too much and too long.

It was some months after we visited Mark that we had a letter telling us that Mark was improved and would be transferred to our county hospital so that he could be nearer home. We were hopeful that his improvement would continue and that he would soon be out of the hospital. When he was returned we went to visit him. Again, we were not prepared for what we saw. He had pulled out nearly all of his hair since we had seen him, a few curly wisps of hair were all that remained on his bald head. His mind was clear. He improved so quickly that it was not long before he was allowed to come home for overnight. He slept in his old room. In the middle of the night he woke up screaming. We were able to quiet him until morning. The next day Roy drove him back to the hospital. I did not want to bring him home often but felt guilty if I didn't. His presence disrupted our lives, a small sacrifice if we were helping our son.

The long nightmare began that continued for eight years. Mark improved so rapidly that the hospital would not keep him. He was sent to a halfway house where he was responsible for himself, had almost complete freedom to come and go. From being totally dependent to being almost totally independent was difficult for him and for us. We wanted to help him when he needed help but at the same time, we wanted to give him the opportunity to exercise his own independence to regain his confidence.

He no longer had a driver's license and began riding a bicycle. He had the bicycle only a short time before it was stolen. He did not have the ability to hold everything together. When he forgot to lock it up, it soon disappeared. He began riding buses and rapid transit as he tried to find work or go to school The daily problems of living were more than he could handle sometimes and he would begin acting crazily as his anxiety increased.

He was unable to sustain himself over time at a job or finish out a quarter at the University where he had enrolled, hoping to continue work on his college degree. He was adamant in his refusal to check in at the hospital long after it was apparent that he was out of control. His brother, Paul, allowed him to move into a house he and a friend, Rick, were renting. "I don't see how Rick put up with Mark as long as he did," Paul told me later.

Paul asked Mark to leave when he discovered that Mark repeatedly forgot to lock up when he left. They could not trust him to be responsible for their property. The long revolving door syndrome began. He was in and out of hospitals, apartments and jails for the next six years.

Our phone rang night and day. Mark's desperate voice would plead with us to rescue him from somewhere. When we decided, after years of vacillation, to get a phone with an unlisted number, Mark could no longer reach us. He would come by more often or send someone to relay a message. He found people in strange places who were willing to rescue him. One day, a man we did not know came over to tell us that Mark wanted us to bail him out of jail. When we refused to give him the money for the bail, he was shocked.

"How can you do that to your own son? I couldn't do it."

"I know," I replied, "Most people wouldn't." Though I was confident of my decision, it was not easy to bear the judgment of others. I was practicing "tough love". If there was going to be any hope for our son, he would have to learn to stay out of the kind of trouble that landed him in jail. If he couldn't learn that, he belonged in a hospital, not on the street.

It was only a matter of a few days before Mark was transferred to the hospital once more. If we had bailed him out he would have wandered the streets and caused more trouble before he could have been incarcerated. It was our conviction that he needed to be institutionalized since he demonstrated repeatedly that he could not take care of himself. Our problem was not only that he could not take care of himself. We were also haunted by the fear that he would cause tragic injury to himself or others before he could be held responsible for his behavior. We had concrete evidence that he was getting into some kind of trouble when we began, over the years, receiving ambulance bills one after another. After a few years, if Mark were not locked up somewhere, every time I heard a police siren I would become tense and wonder if he was in trouble.

In those days, the criteria for releasing a person to the street were simple. If the person had a place to go or said he did and could say his name and address himself, the judge would release him to the street. There was no regulation requiring him to look at the records of that person. Mark was able to look very rational and learned how to respond, so that he was frequently released when he was hardly able to keep himself together long enough to remember if he had eaten his last meal. Because of his clever manipulation, he was able to release himself for a year during which he remained at large and lived mostly in the street.

A difficult and trying time for us all. He bothered his brother and sister, Beth, who lived in the area, disrupting their households when he wasn't harassing us. He tried his best to work, to find a place to live but each time he succeeded, he would soon be evicted.

Since his most recent release to the streets, I had not seen Mark for a number of days. I came home from a meeting one day and found him waiting for me on the porch. He looked drawn as if he hadn't been sleeping. I knew he was not taking care of himself. Damn it, just when I was feeling halfway up for a change, there he was again.

"I've been kicked out of my place," he said.

"What will you do?" I asked.

"I don't know." He looked forlorn as he had looked so many times before, this son who had been so confident and able only a short time ago. I didn't know what to do. I couldn't help him and I couldn't take him in and he had no place to go. As he drove away in the car he had bought since he had managed to obtain his driver's license, I knew that I could not go on without some help for myself.

This saga had no end. It repeated over and over and over until I felt hope vanishing. I wanted to be free of this. I was ready to let him sink but he would not leave us alone. He appeared over and over at the house. How he had managed, I don't know. He found an old car. Maybe he lived in it. One day he came by and asked if he could have some breakfast. I fixed him something when he told me he had picked up a hitchhiker who was waiting in his car. I did not want to see his passenger even when Mark had suggested he invite him in. It was enough to look at my homeless bedraggled son. He was visibly agitated and close to breaking. When he left to go, I was relieved only momentarily for he rushed back into the house. Running for the phone he yelled, "That bastard drove off with my car and everything I own is in the trunk. I have to call the police."

I had withdrawn phoning privileges because he had abused them so often. Under the circumstances I agreed to let him phone. When he finished phoning he left and I did not hear from him again for days.

There were many other incidents during the ten years before Mark was finally declared incompetent enough to be hospitalized permanently. I felt that I was on the edge of breaking at times. Prior to Mark's breakdown I had completed a process called the Fisher-Hoffman Process, which was claimed to be a therapy to end all therapies. In the thirteen-week intensive process, I dealt with all the residual problems remaining around my father and my own struggle with depression and suicidal thoughts. I felt that I would never need another therapist. With my journal and deep spiritual connection, I believed that I could go it alone. When I began my menopause, it was exacerbated by the stress, and I felt I needed help once again. Even though I did not confide in anyone, I felt crazy inside sometimes. In my journal I wrote, "Mental illness is all around me. I dwell daily, constantly on aberration see it everywhere and I worry. I dream of chaos and I fear for myself. Long ago, right after Mark's illness when I went to EST for six days, I experienced catatonia. The interesting thing was that no one wanted to be around me, it was so threatening to them. I knew that I was whole inside; that the outer manifestation of what looked crazy was only external. I knew I was O.K. Something changed after that. I lost my old self, that self that can control and keep me together. I am truly a little crazy. I wouldn't see crazy everywhere if it weren't in me." Then I wrote something that felt grounding and I went on with my day normally.

"Dark dark night—dark days. You descend on me leaving me without joy and light. I must remain in the dark and one day, a new life will emerge and I will once again be reminded of the season of dying and rising, the dying and rising, the cyclical nature of the universe and the cyclical nature of me."

Fear for my own health prodded me to find a doctor. When I went to one he told me that I should be taking hormones. I didn't want to take hormones. There wasn't enough evidence that they are safe. I argued with him and looked for another doctor only to hear the same advice. I resisted hormones and continued to suffer sleepless nights as I woke ten or more times a night drenched in sweat. I was sure that if the tension diminished, the symptoms would do the same. How could I alleviate the stress?

We were at a Christmas party when I began a conversation with an attractive woman about my age. When I learned she was a psychiatrist I told her that I was looking for a doctor that didn't believe in hormones. I was looking for relief some other way. She told me that she had success treating smoke addiction and menopausal symptoms with acupuncture and Chinese herbs. She agreed with me about hormones and said she seldom recommended them.

Relieved to find her I began working with her almost at once. We worked together for a year until once more I felt stabilized and able to manage. We both agreed that there wasn't much more she could do for me. From that time on, no matter what Mark did I had learned to cope on my own.

Whenever things would stabilize for a while with Mark, we would begin to hope that he would recover. Those times did not happen often but were frequent enough to keep us vacillating between giving up and hoping. Like a seesaw I wavered between hope and hopelessness. I thought of the poet, T.S. Eliot, "Wait without hope for hope would be hope for the wrong thing." I struggled within myself to keep my optimistic outlook so that I did not radiate despair to those around me. I began to leave the house as often as I could, since if Mark came he would go away if I were not there. One day he came by and saw me go to the neighbors. I had locked the house as I left. From next door I heard the sound of breaking glass. I ran home. He had broken the window on the back door.

"Why the hell do you have to lock up when you just run to the neighbors?" he demanded. "This is my home. Can't I come in when I want to?"

I was raging inside as I took a deep breath and said calmly, "Mark, this is not your home anymore. You will have to fix the window."

He fixed the window that very day. I was ambivalent about requiring him to repair the window. I would as soon have him leave because I knew he should be at his job. It was incidents like those that kept him and me in a constant state of agitation and pressed our endurance to the limit.

That fall I found myself cringing every time the doorbell or phone rang. I heard bells in my sleep. I became jumpy and nervous in my waking hours and had nightmares when I slept. I wrote in my journal, "I need to get out of here, be with normal, sane people. I will go crazy dwelling on aberration and waiting for the next crisis. I have spent my life shoring up knowledge, answers so that I would have an answer for every dilemma."

By the time I had finished my college degree in psychology and human development, I had gained considerable experience as a counselor. I had been leading women's support groups, couples communication groups with my husband and alone. When Mark broke down, I was investigating further training. Disturbed by his illness, I was ambivalent about wanting to listen to people's problems but listening to theirs took me out of my own, however briefly. With Mark coming into the office or breaking in upon us in our home, there was no place where I felt safe from his intrusive behavior.

I was home one morning listening to the radio when I heard the announcer say that the public schools were looking for substitute teachers. With only a college degree and no experience as a teacher, I applied and was accepted. They were so desperate that they were taking people with two years of college. What drew me more than interest in the work itself was the fact that I would have someplace away from the house where Mark would not be able to find me. All those hours would be guaranteed Mark free.

The work was difficult and exhausting but it was better than being home. I liked the children and tried to make the day as interesting as I could for them.

As a substitute I often was called to difficult classrooms. My menopausal symptoms were aggravated so that I was often drenched in sweat as I stood before the class. There were dangers in the classroom. I found no place to hide.

One day I went into a class in which there was a large mentally retarded boy. The principal warned me to be careful as he might become violent.

All day I was careful not to aggravate the boy. When we gathered for our afternoon story, I asked the children to form a circle around me and when he refused, I touched his hand inviting him to come. He jerked his hand away and lunged at me. I ducked. He picked up some books and began throwing them as he tried to get his hands around my neck. The children, fourth graders, were smaller than the boy and terrified, they ran for cover.

"Letita, run to the office and get the principal," I ordered as I pushed open the classroom door and held it successfully against this strong angry boy until help arrived.

The principal was sorry about my experience but was glad that he could report that the boy was a danger. He told me later, "I've been try-ing for all year to get this boy transferred out of this school. He doesn't belong in a normal class. He is too volatile. Now maybe he will be put where he belongs."

I was sorry, and I hoped the boy would find happiness somewhere else. Where would I find a less stressful place for myself?

The work was so exhausting that by the weekend I hardly did a thing but rest up for the next week. After handling the issue of our sick son and teaching, I had little reserve for anything else. When after two years of teaching I thought about whether I should go back, I was grateful when my husband discouraged me from doing it. I really didn't want to go back but for want of some other alternative, I was tempted. The ups and downs with Mark were constant.

"You'll find something to do. It's such trying work, and you get so tired. I don't know why you would want to go back." Roy said.

The urge to run away pursued me. I could hardly bear a day at home. Sometimes when the doorbell would ring, I would hide and hope that whoever it was would go away. I felt like a prisoner in my own house. We began going away on weekends and I told our pastor, "You won't see us in church because we have to get out of town whenever we are free to go. We're going to our country place at least three Sundays a month." I did lit-erally run away for years.

I was running off on a ski trip one weekend when our daughter, Beth, called. "I'm going to the hospital. Don't you want to know if we're having a boy or a girl?" she said. We had met her at the hospital for one false alarm and by this time I wanted to get away more than I wanted to know about our first grandchild. "I can wait. I'll call from the mountains. Besides, you may not have the baby before we return."

I had heard that being a grandparent was wonderful. Now I knew it was true. Seeing our eldest daughter with her child, my grandchild, in her arms has to be one of the sweetest scenes I shall ever witness. I had never had grandparents and all my pictures of a grandmother I had created in my mind. I became the kind of grandmother I would have liked to have. I found pleasure and joy in being with our little girl and put aside a day each week either to go to see her or invite our daughter to bring her over. By the time she was six months old, she came to me as readily as she went to her mother, and we became fast friends. When I wasn't crying for pain, I was crying for joy. Perhaps the joy I felt over Allie was enhanced because of the pain I had been experiencing for so long. I was utterly grateful, stunned and speechless at times at the wonder of that child.

For the next two years, Mark continued in and out of the hospital. Sometimes he was in jail. He lost his belongings and would have to start over. His glasses were broken, and he would have no means to buy new ones. He was unable to manage his life. The simplest problems became insurmountable for him. He created new problems faster than he could solve old ones. For example, he got a job and went out to buy a car to get to work. It was an old car that looked good but hardly a week went by before the car blew up one day on the freeway. One day he said to me when he had returned from being in jail, "Mom, it wasn't so bad there. I think you suffer worse than I do." Hearing those words gave me temporary relief. I found it hard to believe that he was not suffering from all the things that were happening to him.

Before he became so difficult and unpredictable that I would not have him in the house, I would let Mark stay with us a few days at a time when he was without housing. He was homeless often, and when he did find a place to live, he would be evicted. No one seemed to be able to live with him for long.

When he slept at our house I would lock our bedroom door at night. I did not want to have him bursting in waking me out of a sleep if he had a nightmare. When Mark discovered one night that our door was locked, I found the following note under my door the next morning.

"I'm not going to beat you up even though you may want to beat me up. I don't blame you. I know I'm a real bastard. I can't help it though. It is my outlook on life that makes me that way. I do love you though and I don't want you to be afraid of me. Love, Paul."

He had signed his brother's name. I felt sad when I read his note. His handwriting was deteriorated. It used to be neat and legible. I answered him thus:

"Dear Mark,

Here is a key while you are here. I feel more secure if the doors are well locked. I suppose I am afraid quite a bit but I try not to be. Thank you for your note. I do not think you are a bastard though sometimes you act like one. Love, Mom."

We wished Mark would stay out of our lives, stop pulling us into all his problems, which we were helpless to solve. He did not leave us alone. He continued to come by the house often looking for materials for a job or to see if we had something he needed. I tried to discourage him by getting his things out. Still he came.

Our first grandson had been born. I was all prepared to go to Denver to help our daughter, Deborah and to see her child. One day before I was due to leave Mark came by. Our three-year old granddaughter, Allie, was with me, and my best friend had stopped by. We were enjoying the morning when Mark showed up and I was annoyed at the intrusion wishing he would leave. He handed me a stuffed toy, "I brought this for Allie," he said. Then he pushed his way into the house and went down the basement before I could ask him what he wanted. While I waited for him to leave, I listened. What was he taking? Should I go check? I called down. "What are you getting, Mark?"

"I need some paint for this job," he said.

"There's nothing of yours there." I called. When he did not leave I became impatient and went down the basement to urge him on out. He kept looking in the paint cupboard. Thinking only of myself, I failed to read the signs. He was taut as a violin string, not unusual for him, though I had seldom seen him so agitated and still in control of himself. When he opened the door to finally leave, I gave in to the impulse to push him out. The instant I touched him he turned on me, picked up a brick outside the door and hurled it through the basement window. I ran for the stairs grabbed Allie, told my friend to follow as I ran to our upstairs bedroom and locked the door. Mark did not follow me but went on a window-breaking rampage. Handing the child to my friend, I pushed them into the windowless closet while below a window broke in my study. I phoned for the police then joined the others to huddle in the closet until the sound of breaking glass ceased, and I heard the car drive off. By the time he stopped breaking windows, seventeen windows including two large picture windows and frames were smashed.

The policewoman that answered my call was small and slight. She appeared shocked and frightened. Trying to be business-like she scolded me angrily. "If you will just stop shaking and tell me what happened," she said, "maybe we can get a report of this."

Teeth chattering, I stammered, "I'm trying."

Her questions served to calm me as we worked on her report. By the time she finished we were able to converse rationally. She was thoughtful as she said, "I wonder if he is the young blonde man I saw standing in the rain yesterday morning without anything on his head, without a jacket, looking lost.

Holding back the tears as best I could, I replied, "It could have been."

The noise of the breaking glass must have alerted every neighbor that was home for blocks. Though no one ever talked about it to us, or offered sympathy, I felt shame and humiliation in the neighborhood for weeks. Even if they had not heard, everyone could see and would tell others what they knew. Some of our windows would be boarded up for a month before new ones could be made and installed. Our immediate neighbors felt more fear for themselves than sympathy for us, which I could understand. Who wouldn't be afraid of this violent person?

Our house was like a minefield that week. Every room was strewn with shattered glass. There was no safe place upstairs or down. We found shards of glass for weeks and months and even years later I found slivers under the carpet. My plans to go to Denver were canceled, as it was necessary to remain in the house at all times until the windows could be replaced. Tape and boards were used to shut out the wind and rain but our house would have been an easy target for burglars.

A few days later, when I recovered from the initial shock I called our pastor. "Could you and Mildred come over? Something terrible has happened." I said. He called back. "We'll be over tonight. Eight o'clock?"

When they arrived, I told them what had happened. "You can see the mess we're in with all these broken windows." Though it was dark and the boarded windows were not as noticeable as when the light of day was shut out, they had only to look to see the devastation around us.

"Mark did this two days ago. I'm still reeling from the shock. I thought the four of us could bring some kind of healing to the situation with prayer or something so that this evil that has befallen us does not darken this house, my home. You know, some kind of exorcism, or something." It was a relief to talk about what had happened. Everyone in the neighborhood had been silent. We shared how difficult it was. I asked God to keep us through the dark days and to help us all. As we felt the love and support of dear friends, the burden lightened and my attitude changed. The anger and rage that I had been experiencing for years evaporated. With the realization that we were dealing with illness, not rebellion, came a new sense of the tragedy that had entered our lives. I felt overwhelming compassion for Mark; that he should be saddled with such a destiny. In my journal I wrote, "The terror has subsided. I am in touch with anguish for Mark and a new realization that there is no security such as I had been believing in. And what about these rights that I have been screaming, (Have I no rights?) Maybe I have none; that all I have and am comes from God and any moment may be snatched away." It would be misleading to say that I did not become angry anymore. My journal is replete with records of raging moods. What had changed was that I no longer felt anger toward Mark. I sometimes raged at God for visiting such a fate upon us all, and especially felt sorry for myself for I felt I had been given an unfair dose of mental illness in my lifetime. At the same time I raged, I would also offer up thanks for the good things of which there were many.

When the windows were secured I left for Denver. Sorry to have to tell our daughter, Deborah, about the windows, it would have been impossible to keep it from her had I been able to do so. She had always been sensitive to feelings and would pick them up easily. If Roy and I had been fighting and we pretended nothing was wrong, she would say, "You and dad are in a fight," or "You're mad at daddy, aren't you?" It was bitter news I bore to her happy household. Despite the devastation that I left behind, I was able sometimes to forget about what awaited me at home and enjoyed Deborah's child along with her. Many times in our lives the bitter followed the sweet in an unending circle.

In my journal I wrote, "There are gains for all our losses, there are balms for all our pains." I refused to be crushed by the actions and disasters of one person. We had three other children that gave us support and love. As the grandchildren arrived my capacity for loving became unblocked and I felt love surging through me whenever I thought of one of our little ones. I wrote:

Life may flood us with vicissitudes
For days, months and even years

Until our hope for better days
Lay shattered on the ground.
Then, quite unexpectedly,
It will shower upon us such an abundance of blessings,
The like of which we had not expected,
Hoped for nor deserve.
In our gratitude, we are stunned and speechless.

As I gradually came to an acceptance of Mark's illness and realized, despite the prayers and hope of friends and loved ones, he was hopelessly ill, I felt an ache in my heart that would not give way. I asked my doctor one day, "Do you believe in a broken heart? Literally, I mean. My heart aches all the time."

"Yes, I do I think there can be some physical manifestation of heartbreak." she said.

"Well, if it can break, it can heal," I said hopefully. I longed for healing and for an end to the pain.

There was no respite from the pain. When we did not hear from Mark for a number of days, we knew he was either in the hospital or in jail. We tried to go on with our lives normally during the silent periods but what looked like normal on the outside was not so at all. Hardly a day passed that I did not worry and think of Mark. My dreams would remind me that Mark was part of me should I cease to think about him however briefly.

One day we had a letter telling us that Mark would be transferred to the hospital out of the area and was presently in the local hospital. I drove over to visit him before he was transferred. I found him with his jaws wired shut.

"He had it broken in jail." the attendant told me. "I've seen him many times in and out of here but this time he was more disturbed than I have seen him before."

When the wires were removed from his jaw and he was able to speak, I asked him what had happened.

"Well, Mom, you know those guys don't know how to speak English. They needed some lessons. I did the "rain in Spain" number on them. They didn't like it. This is what I got for my pains," I remembered our staff psychiatrist saying, "They just don't have any sense of appropriateness, don't use good judgment." How true. Mark, a blonde white man taunting a prison cell full of black men about their use of the English language. Even as I suffered with him, I had to laugh. Once in a while things became so ridiculous that I was torn between laughter and tears.

Chapter VII.

We were into the seventh year of Mark's breakdown. We had endured one crisis after another and still I resisted accepting that our son was a victim of schizophrenia and that there was no hope for his recovery. I was gradually coming around and even able to speak of him to others without breaking into tears or feeling miserable for hours after thinking about him. I called my younger brother to see how things were going with him on the farm. I felt a need to make a connection with my childhood family and home. I was ready to talk a bit about Mark. "I think I have come to accept that Mark will never be well. Finally." I said.

"I guess that's the hardest part, accepting it," he replied. I wondered how he knew. What has he had to accept in his life? We have had so little contact, I had no idea what pain and suffering he has endured. Not knowing lulled me into thinking he had none. Miles and years separated us. We hadn't been very close. Yet this time I felt heard and cared about. I needed all the support I could find.

I said to my husband on a good day, "I can't believe how well I have been. I hardly even get a cold. With all the sleepless nights and tension we have endured, I have often wondered why my body has not broken down in some way, at least with the flu or something."

Along the way there were so many things to affirm and for which to be thankful. Though they were overshadowed by the illness of our son, it would be unfair to leave them out of the story. There was the celebration of our twenty-seventh wedding anniversary the same year of Roy's twenty-fifth year of ordination. There were the weddings of our two daughters, the graduation from college of our youngest son, my earning my bachelor's degree the same year Roy was awarded his doctor of ministry degree. There were celebrations of our friends, weddings, baptisms, going away parties and travel.

The words of the poet mystic, St. John of the Cross, echoed in my head, "For love gives power to my life however black and blind my day." There was love around me when I could feel and accept it.

We went to the Caribbean one-year, to Hawaii another. There were professional conferences where we met with friends of many years and shared joys and sorrows with one another. We knew we were not alone in our pain. Every joy we had in the family I wished Mark could share. Most important of all those years was the birth of our four grandchildren, three girls and a boy. Though Mark knew and loved Beth's children, Allie and Jennie, he has never had an opportunity to meet and know Deborah's children, Matthew and Sarah. Every time that Deborah has been home he has been either too ill or locked up somewhere. With children he is able to express his love and tenderness. The last time we planned to visit with the children, we called the hospital to find that he was in restraints.

Despite the passage of time and the good things that have come our way, I still discover my childhood reaction when things got tough: "I'm going to run away." The problem is that there is no running away from oneself. Running away seemed to run in the family definitely. My father used to run away and hide. Mark began running away from himself. For years he kept busy so as not to look within himself. He was always on the run. I was somewhat the same way, always finding something to do, not stopping to be. When I stopped wanting to get away from problems, I began literally to "run away" from home to escape the immediate emotional involvement and the pain of Mark's problems about which I seemed helpless to do anything but suffer.

I was so tired of running. I wished that we could resolve something once and for all, when one day I realized that there is no "once and for all." Life is just a series of events, many of which are happy and some of which we wish would go away and are sad and difficult. I began to learn to take a day at a time. I must be handling the stress pretty well. Wasn't my health good? I was able to substitute teach in the public schools as a way of involving myself outside the home. That took a lot of energy, but it kept me from getting inordinately depressed. I could ski, dance, swim, play tennis and do my daily work. But was I healthy inside? Apparently not. While I was going from day to day marveling at how my health was holding so that I didn't even get a cold, my body was doing something else.

It was the eighth year of Mark's illness. Roy and I were getting ready to go skiing. We loved to ski and when all four children were teen-agers at once and I needed to let go and let them be, when I went to the mountains I could drop all cares and concerns for them as we careened down those magnificent slopes in the high Sierras. Maybe it would do the same for me now. Anxious to be off, I was going to ignore a warning sign when my intuition prodded me to act.

I noticed blood on my underwear. Though I had not had menstrual periods for a few years I did not think it unusual for a woman to show blood again. I had been exercising heavily and attributed the bleeding to that. About to dismiss the sign as insignificant, I remembered that I had also had severe stomach cramps for which I could find no explanation. "Maybe I'll just call the hospital and let them know," I thought. The advice nurse told me to come in. "We're going skiing. I'll come in when I return." I said. "How old are you?" she asked. When I told her she ordered, "You get in here today." By the tone of her voice she knew something I didn't know, though I was confident that it would not be serious.

I acquiesced. "Oh, all right. But I know it is nothing."

When I went in, inwardly fussing because of the nuisance this was when I was planning something else, the doctor took a biopsy and told me to go ahead and go skiing. I was relieved for my immediate concern was that he would tell me I could not exercise. More concerned about breaking a leg skiing than I was over the results of the test, I went off with Roy to some of the best snow of the season and enjoyed our two days carefree and lighter than I had been for years.

The first thing I found when I returned was a registered letter from the hospital asking me to call the hospital upon my return. There was another message on the recorder, "Urgent! Call the hospital." On the phone the doctor said, "We want you to come in, maybe you will need to have a D & C. I had heard of the D & C from other women but did not know what it was, again, I didn't think it was something to get too concerned about. When I reported to the doctor's office, a woman walked in. She was a doctor I had not seen before. With only a brief greeting she looked at me and said, "You have cancer." "No way," I retorted. "There's no cancer in my family. You've obviously made some mistake. In any event, I want a second opinion." To cover my shock I made a demand that already I knew was ridiculous. She was sure, I could tell. Her approach may have been brutal but it was clear. In my whole life I had never expected to hear that word relating to me. I had become used to "crazy" but not cancer. I had never expected to hear that word applied to me. People die from cancer, have radiation treatments and then die, suffer endless days of misery. Haven't I had enough? Not cancers!

"We already have a second opinion and a third. We all agree it is cancer. We're just not agreed on what kind. We'll do another biopsy. Do you think you can stand it?" Was she doing this for herself or for me?

"Next to what you've just told me, what is a little biopsy? Of course I can stand it! Do what you have to do." Always before I had been distant and avoided doctors, not giving them much power to tell me what to do. I was a healthy woman with minor medical problems who knew how to take care of herself. Suddenly I was clay in this doctor's hands. Cancer was something I wasn't going to argue about and something about which I knew nothing. I had to trust the medical profession completely for the first time in my life. I was even glad they were there for me.

"Well, I guess my cells finally broke down from all the stress I have been under for many years," I said matter-of-factly. At least I knew what had caused this monster.

"Stress doesn't cause cancer," she said.

Right then I knew she didn't know much about the psychological effects of stress upon the immune system. This was no time to educate her. "Well, let's not argue about what caused it or decide who is right. Let's get the damn stuff out!" I said emphatically. I knew when I said "damn" that I was pretty angry, but I tried to sound cool and remain calm. We both laughed. The tension lifted and we went on to discuss what would happen next. The longer we talked the more confident I felt that I would be in good hands with this woman and was glad when she said she would be doing the surgery.

While I was calm in the doctor's office, I did not maintain that calm for long.

I was angry about everything. That doctor! Everyone knows that stress could upset the body's ability to cope with disease and infection. The range of frustration, anger, resentment, grief, unresolved worry are more severe an assault on the body than physical injury and harder to diagnose and treat. Effects of physical stress are mild compared to the ravages of emotional stress. I should know. Lord knows I had had an inordinate amount for a prolonged period of time. Where did this doctor train? I vented my anger silently at the doctor because I didn't know how else to deal with the various emotions that assailed me. Anger was one that I was competent to express.

Not yet ready to deal with the fear and the grief, I still focused on the doctor's lack of knowledge. Never mind. She's young and her fixed points of view are important to her security. Maybe when she has had more experience she will be able to listen to her patients and alter her opinions appropriately. Small matter. I liked her and I was determined to have a positive hopeful attitude by the time I entered surgery. I knew that positive imaging was known to affect positive outcome. There was a lot of anger to process before that time arrived.

I wrote in my Journal one day when I felt so impatient and angry I did not know what else to do to release the emotions.

> "It must always come as a shock to be told
> That you have cancer when you feel so well
> That no one could tell
> That anything was wrong even though you're old,
> And the time has come for your body to begin its dying.
> It's just that you don't expect it today
> Nor did you dream it would come in this way.
> You find yourself pleading and crying
> For mercy, reprieve from your fate.
> You ask for more years
> And release from the fears
> That the cancer was discovered too late.
> Your life will never be the same
> Once your disease has had a name.

If it wasn't good poetry, it was good therapy. I felt better after focusing my energies on the writing instead of obsessing in my raw feelings constantly. I knew they had to be processed, whatever they were, but the writing gave me some temporary relief. I felt as if I could not bear any more pain or sorrow in my life. Mark's ongoing illness was a constant pain.

One evening I fumed to my husband, "It's too much, just too much! I get everything." I was even mad at him that he was well. "It's not fair!" I was angry and afraid. Afraid I would die. We had no way of knowing how far the cancer had spread until surgery so I had only to hope and wait, knowing that all my hoping and prayers for the outcome were in vain. The die had been cast. I lived in this state for only two weeks. Though Roy and I had planned to go to a church convention to see old friends, I did not want to reveal that I had cancer for I was ashamed as if I had caused it and was worthy of judgment. Knowing we would have to face the unknown when I returned, I opted to schedule the surgery instead of taking the trip.

"Don't you want any support?" my husband asked when I told him. I did not want him to tell anyone but our children that I had cancer. I could feel the shame even with him. I knew he was right and that I should not withhold this information from people that cared about me. There was no need to go it alone. When I told friends and added my name to the prayer list at church, I received warm and tender messages from many people who otherwise would have been deprived of the opportunity to respond to me and show me they cared. I was surprised at the number of others who revealed to me that they, too, had had cancer. Then they would share encouraging facts about their experience.

Some journal entries prior to surgery: "Yesterday I felt angry and ripped off about having cancer. Nearly everyone I talked to said something that made me angry and sorry for myself. Everything was grist for my reaction mill. I was afraid, for the first time in my life that this might be the time for me to die. I knew how afraid I was when I dreamed my sister (who is a nurse and sees cancer all the time and speaks with authority on the subject) called me on the phone. She said, 'you are dying. That pain in your stomach proves that you are dying.' I woke drenched in sweat and woke my husband who comforted me as best he could. It was hard for him to cover his concern that he might lose me. I was glad we would not have long to wait until we knew what to expect.

My friend, Jean, called. "What can I do for you?" she asked. I hesitated.

I could feel the anger rise thinking; "Everyone is being so kind because they are relieved it isn't them." I held my tongue.

"I was wondering if you would like to come out for a hot tub and do a hypnosis session in preparation for surgery?"

She is a therapist with a specialty in relaxation and hypnosis. "Yes, I would. That sounds wonderful. I would like to program out the negative emotions."

I was surprised at my own positive response and noticed that my negative feelings diminished with my expressed intention.

Jean spent two hours with me in hypnosis programming positive thoughts following the hot tub. I returned home relaxed and confident.

Our children called expressing love and concern. From Denver Deborah said, "I'm coming home, Mom. When do you want me, before or after the surgery?" Unused to such attention, I cried at her thoughtfulness. I knew that she had her child and her job to consider as well as my wishes. Those days I was easily overcome with emotion. Paul, who is independent and sometimes distant, called and came to see me.

We sat and shelled nuts for two hours and talked. Mark was able to hold himself together long enough to come by and express his concern. Our oldest daughter, Beth was willing to do anything I needed.

"Do you want me to bring the girls in to see you?" she asked.

Of course I did and she did. When I thought of my life being over the thought of not seeing the grandchildren grow up was foremost in my mind. They were always such a source of delight and joy to me.

For the two weeks preceding the surgery, life was normal. Roy had a wedding to perform. We invited the young couple for dinner while they went over plans for the wedding. As I listened to them planning for their future I felt a twinge of bitterness at what my "future" had brought. Roy and I made a date to play tennis once more.

"It may be a while before we can play again," he said.

I filled the days. Our good friends came over for dinner and played bridge with us. The busy-ness would not allay fully the anxiety and the anger. I wrote in my journal.

"I had a long talk with Sarah. I felt angry that she is older and never had cancer. I am furious that I have had such a miserable menopause, angry that Mark broke down on my fiftieth birthday and that I have cancer at fifty-seven. This is no time to call my friends. This is a time to be inward. I am weepy. I don't like having cancer in my body. I want a healthy whole body. Well, so much for today."

Once the negative feelings were processed I was able to see and experience the other emotions. I wrote shortly before entering the hospital.

"What shall I render to the Lord for His goodness to me? I will render unto the Lord a cheerful attitude so much as I am able today. I will curb my propensity to self-pity, sadness and rebellion, not suppress those things but curb them, write dialogue, talk to them, whatever it takes to contain them so that I shall reflect, in however small a measure my gratitude for what I do have and have been given. By grace I shall be able to do that.

"If thine eye be single…my single intention is to reflect and project love and acceptance of what is, remembering that scripture tells us that 'All things work together for good for those who love God.' I accept that all that is happening in my life is working for good for all concerned and that were I to see the bigger picture, I should not despair.

"Scripture also says, 'In everything give thanks.' Today I shall give thanks with my whole heart."

Sympathetic to my wishes to have the surgery as soon as possible, "to get the damn stuff out as soon as we can," I was in the hospital within two weeks of finding out I had cancer. When the doctor came into my room the afternoon that I entered the hospital, to see if I had any questions, I asked her why she came in and announced without any prefacing that I had cancer. I told her though it was a shock, I preferred it to having her come and try to soften the truth, which I felt would have been an insult to me and my ability to handle the news.

"Well, I'll tell you," she said, "I have to tell so many people that they have cancer that if I tried to make up a story for each one, I'd get my stories mixed up. That would be more trouble than just putting it out there in all its starkness. There is no way that softening the news will change the harsh facts. I find most people handle it pretty well, even as you did."

"We want to know the truth," I answered, "even if we don't like it." I thought of how long it took me to accept the diagnosis of our son's illness. Because it was difficult to make a clear diagnosis, we argued with the doctors and with ourselves to try to make the diagnosis less damning. With the cancer diagnosis there is nothing to argue about. Cancer is cancer and I had it.

Roy and my friend Lee came to the hospital the night before surgery. Lee read the section on "preparation for surgery" from the hypnosis manual for the second time.

She had come by earlier in the afternoon and read it to me then. By the time I was left alone, I was in a deeply relaxed positive state. On my rock hard bed I dozed off and on through the night, impatient for morning.

Using the positive suggestions, which had been programmed in my subconscious, I came to the operating room with a light heart. As I had been lying on my hard bed during the night I tried to think of how to make a joke with my doctor. When I saw her I first said, "You are confident, relaxed and going to do a perfect job for me." Then, "Do you know why the recovery rate is so high at Kaiser?"

"No, why?" she asked as she was tying her gown.

"Given the choice between another night on the mortuary slabs you call beds and getting well and going home, people choose to get well." I said.

She looked startled rather than amused at the words 'mortuary slab." She missed the joke or did she? My unconscious might have tricked me into revealing that on some level I was afraid of dying despite my confident light mood. She, too, may have been having thoughts about what she would find during the surgery.

When she regained her composure and realized that I was trying to be funny, she said, "It sounds like your bed was pretty hard. Would you like me to order you a softer mattress? I can do that." Before I could answer I was off to a deep sleep, which lasted for eight hours.

Back in my room on my softer bed, hearing voices I opened my eyes and saw Roy, Mark, Paul and Beth standing around my bed. Roy was looking down at me and laughing. All the traces of tension I had seen on his face for days were gone.

"You did just great. Everything went very well. The doctor is pleased and so are we all. Pastor Berg just left."

"Oh," I felt disappointment. "I wish I could have talked to him," I said.

"You did talk to him. You chatted about any number of things. Don't you remember? When he said, as he left, 'God bless you', you replied, 'He has blessed me all over.'"

I had been blessed all over. All the family was around me confirming their love and concern for me. Even Mark was able to be there for me as I had been for him so many times. I was glad to see him and gladder still for this brief insulation from his illness. It would not last long.

I drifted off to sleep and woke later to an empty room. Before I could reflect on what had been happening, the doctor walked in. I would now ask her the question that lurked heavy in my mind, which I feared most to ask.

"Will I need to have radiation treatments?" I asked.

"No, none whatsoever. You can just concentrate on getting well and going home. There was only a little cancer, which had not penetrated to the lining. We are sure we got it all. You should be good as new in no time. You were in such excellent health when you came in, I am sure your recovery will be rapid and complete."

Tears stung my eyes. As much as anything pertaining to the cancer, I had dreaded chemotherapy treatments. I had read and heard so many horrendous things about the side effects that I wanted no part of it. Forgetting that I had ever felt like a victim, I thought my luck better than I deserved and thanked God that very moment.

After five days in the hospital, on Easter Sunday I came home from the hospital to my quiet home. Deborah came two days later and spent hours on my bed talking with me or helping me in the kitchen as we prepared simple meals. In only two weeks I was physically fully recovered to resume an easy regular schedule. When I returned to see the doctor for a three-week check up I asked her if it would be all right to wash my kitchen floor or play tennis. "You can wash your kitchen floor if you feel like it and when you finish you can come do mine, too. As for tennis, okay, do what you feel like doing."

Though I did tire and the hot flashes plagued me, my recovery from cancer was fast and easy. I needed all the strength I could muster for the days ahead.

Mark was having a hard time. He had found a nice place to live but was soon evicted because of his irresponsible behavior. I wrote in my journal.

"It has been like a threatening storm that does not come but does not abate. Mark found a nice place, struggled to get his driver's license back and found work. It lasted such a short time and is now all over. He is homeless and I pity him so much I wish I could take him in." That night I dreamed about him. In the dream I ask my sister if she thinks I ought to give Mark a home and see if he can find healing here. Even as I ask, I know the hopelessness of the idea. I woke crying as I felt the longing to rescue and save him. When I fell back to sleep I dreamed, "We are going on a train and the baby stayed behind. I go back for him and the train goes on without us. I cry in frustration."

I realize that I cannot keep the baby and keep moving in my own life. I have to leave the child behind. It is the old problem of how to let the child go.

When Mark was evicted once more he slept in his car. This time the car was an old broken down vehicle without a door. I hoped that he would be picked up for crazy behavior before he was attacked in his car. It was hard to sleep nights again.

Managing to hold himself together he found work and began to earn enough money that he became confident of himself and his exaggerated sense of what he could do took over. To our surprise he drove up one day in a new truck.

"I bought this $10,000.00 truck, Dad. Isn't it nice?"

He was proud to have a vehicle as nice as his brother's. We were shocked. How did he manage to finance a new car or convince a salesperson that he was a responsible risk? He was so unstable around us. But we had learned to read the signs. I had to remember that he was very good at covering his feelings and could look very normal when it was important for him to do so. I knew we were in for some hard times once more.

We began getting phone calls regarding the truck. Our credit was being checked. Then we had a phone call that Mark was in jail in Reno where he had been driving recklessly and acting bizarre. The truck was in our name, what would we like to do about getting it home? Nothing. We had not bought the truck. Mark had forged our name and managed to get the truck out of the shop by the time the credit check was complete. Over the years he had become proficient in the ways of the street in his desperate efforts to survive. Even as we were furious, we had to laugh. Relieved that Mark had not caused injury to anyone in this last episode, I dreamed one night that "someone in each household was to decide who was to die and who was to live. I was glad that I did not have that responsibility."

When I woke from the dream I thought about how long it had been since I had wished Mark would die. A long time. I no longer wished for anything for him so much as that I should be able to confront the challenges that he presented in my life with courage and wisdom and be able to keep my equilibrium. My prayers were more for me than for anyone else. At least I could do something about myself and finally, after years of hoping, come to see that I was helpless to help Mark.

The waves that the truck episode made did not subside for months though Mark was taken to the hospital from the jail when it was discovered that he was a mental case. For months he was so psychotic that he was in restraints twenty-four hours a day.

In my relief over Mark's hospitalization my grief lightened. When I thought of him in restraints I was comforted by the hope that my friend was right when she said, "Mark isn't in there when he is so crazy. He's not suffering as much as you think."

I know she doesn't know any more than I know if that is true, but it helps me to think it is possible. Even if he were suffering as much as I imagine, I do not want him to get better. Getting better means that he will be released before he is able to manage, as we have witnessed for eight years. We would be in our vicious cycle with its potential for unspeakable tragedy.

We have made contact with the hospital. When Mark became rational we went to see him. I have gone to see him when he is irrational and in restraints. I have learned to bear the pain of seeing our son in all conditions. He is always glad to see me and I to see him. Roy and I are his only links with the outside. He has lost all others.

It will soon be three years since he was finally hospitalized in 1989. His condition is deteriorating visibly. He has lived in an unreal world so long that his real world has died. It does not appear that he shall ever leave the hospital. I am more relieved than upset with such a prediction.

There are families who deal with problems such as we have had with Mark for their whole lifetime. All their energies go into maintaining themselves under unbearable stress. Our ordeal lasted only eight years. I consider myself lucky. I will say, consciously now, "I have been blessed all over."

Chapter VIII.

It was after I had been writing for months about my experience as the mother of Mark that I realized that my work was incomplete. I wanted to put all of this down in a book, but it was too centered on my thoughts and feelings to be useful to anyone but myself. I needed something from the other members of the family. Roy and I had talked over the years but I had not given ear to the children. Until now I was not ready to hear their side.

When I thought of asking the children to talk to me about their experience during Mark's illness, I felt some trepidation. Would they be willing to dredge up old feelings, deal with present ones or would they refuse to talk with me about Mark? I decided to test my idea first on Paul who was most available. I invited him to dinner one night when Roy was away.

"Paul, I want you to come to dinner. Could you spare the whole evening as there is something important I want to talk about with you?"

"I could come Tuesday. If that is okay, what time do you want me?" he said.

Paul's first remark when he walked in was, "What do you want me to fix?"

I wasn't surprised since Paul was handy with so many things I often depended on him to fix broken light switches, replace burned out electric coils on appliances and even install appliances for me. Since he had moved out on his own, I had not asked such favors of him often. I felt he had enough to do taking care of his own household.

"I don't want you to fix anything," I laughed. "What I do want may be less acceptable to you than a request to fix a broken something. But let's have dinner before we talk about what I called you for."

I wasn't anxious to tell him. I felt my anxiety rise through dinner. Maybe I should have told him what I had planned. Would he feel tricked and/or manipulated and then refuse to talk with me at all? I just didn't know how to predict his reaction. We had avoided, as much as possible, talking about Mark when we were together. His situation and illness had never been an acceptable topic of conversation to us either as a family or as individual members, except for Roy and me who could not seem to stop talking and thinking about Mark as we tried to make sense out of what was happening and as we struggled with our own responsibility toward this wayward son. For years we were all too raw from the frequent and immediate crisis' we were called upon to handle to want to deal with talking about those ordeals unless it was absolutely imperative.

"I told you I am writing a book." I said.

"Yes, I think that is a good idea," he replied probably wondering what that had to do with him.

"As I worked on the material I realized how much was missing when I could not honestly write about how it has been for the other members of the family. I would like to talk about what it has been like for you since Mark's illness."

I was grateful and surprised that he responded positively. When we went into the living room after dinner, he stretched out in the chair. He was the picture of confidence in his fashionable clothes. I commented on how handsome he looked. My anxiety vanished. He was showing no signs of resisting my questions.

"I don't dress like this every day. I was seeing clients today," he explained. Paul is a successful engineer with his own company.

"Well what is it you want to know, Mom?" he asked. "If you had some specific questions it would be easier for me."

"Tell me about what it has been like for you with Mark these last years since his breakdown. Maybe you could just begin anywhere." I said. I tape-recorded his recollections.

As if he had been waiting for permission to talk about it all along, Paul launched in without hesitancy or holding back. It was the competition between him and his brother that came to mind first.

"If I would compete with him and he would lose, he would get so mad. You know how he was. He would be so enraged and scream if he lost. He always had to win. You know that. This is the way it was from early on, not necessarily after his illness. We never had a good brother relationship. At times it was okay but most of the time it wasn't. I don't think I noticed any mental illness until he went off the deep end. I just think we weren't close for siblings. I always just thought that was Mark. Maybe you had a better feeling for what was normal and saw things we didn't see," Paul looked thoughtfully at me, maybe asking me to help him make sense out of what he couldn't understand. At the same time my hope was that talking with Paul would increase my understanding.

"Oh, no, I, too, thought that his behavior was just normal behavior for a young man growing up during the turbulent sixties with the violence, the wars, that we lived through. Then there were the changes in the moral fiber of our country with our president betraying us and our heroes turning into villains, or worse yet, criminals. Who could tell, in those days, what was normal? I thought that Dad and I did a good job of keeping stability in our family and, therefore, expected all of you children to come through those years unscathed." I laughed at what now seemed like sheer naiveté. I went on.

"In my wildest dreams, I would not have thought that anyone in our family could become so crazy. From my own success, I had confidence in the current therapies, that we could always get the kind of help we needed for emotional problems and thus avert any serious mental problems among us. I never entertained a notion that together Dad and I couldn't make it turn out for you children. Nor did I imagine that what happened to my father would be repeated with one of my children. When you live so close to someone it is hard to say at what point one recognizes when behavior you're seeing is, in fact, not normal but illness."

Paul listened intently then stretched and yawned, showing little or no emotion.

"That's true," he said. "I didn't think of him as ill until he began being totally off the wall, hearing voices and having incredible fantasies. Then you never knew if he was fabricating the fantasies for effect. Even before his breakdown he had ridiculous ideas of grandeur so I didn't think too much about his weird ideas.

"No matter what he attempted, he was always determined to be the best. He would figure out how he could get around the discipline required to achieve that goal. He had such a low threshold for frustration. He was never able to hold a job. He couldn't work for other people. I don't know why that was, could never figure out what made it so hard for him to work for someone else because he got along with people well when they worked for him.

"Now I just don't have any feeling for him. I feel sorry for him. He's pitiful at this point.

You know he lived with me for a while when he was in and out of the hospital. His irresponsibility was really hard for me to take. He would leave doors unlocked when he left the house. He would come in and make noise at all hours. He never seemed to be able to think or feel how it was for anyone but himself. I'm surprised that my housemate, Rick, put up with him as long as he did. Yeah, that time was really rough." As he shifted restlessly in his chair I guessed that he was holding in some feelings. Trained as an engineer, he is more comfortable explaining and analyzing problems; both are ways of avoiding feelings he did not easily express. Sensing his agitation, I waited quietly.

In a loud voice he went on, emphasizing his words, "I had so many things of value in my house, my electronic equipment, my stereo and all my personal things. I was in constant dread of losing my things. Still I was torn between kicking Mark out and giving him shelter in the hope that he would get on his feet and get going again as he had in the past. I hung on as long as I could stand it. You may be sure I was sorely tried but I didn't want to say anything to you and Dad because I knew you had enough to handle and besides, there wasn't anything you could do."

As I listened, I wondered how many times in the past he had kept his problems to himself because he thought we had enough to handle or could do nothing about them. I felt sadness for having missed a closeness that we might have had. Sensing that he was finished, I approached another aspect of our subject.

"Do you feel ashamed to have a brother who is mentally ill?" I asked.

"Well, everybody that met Mark kinda knew what to expect. He caused a lot of trouble where I worked. They called the police on him several times." he said.

Wondering if he was avoiding talking about feelings of shame, I posed the same question with another word. I relaxed, as I knew when I listened to the recording of this conversation I could listen for nuances I might miss.

"Didn't that humiliate you?"

"Well, not that much. It turns out that they just took it in stride after awhile. It happened so often that most everyone I talked with sympathized and had someone in their family that had similar problems. They all had one or two ghosts of their own. People at work were very supportive of me. I never felt any threat for my job." He paused.

It was so inconceivable to me that Paul would have felt no shame or embarrassment over his brother's many disruptive appearances at his work that I pressed him once more.

"I just thought everyone was ashamed of mental illness in their family. I surely felt that way over my father and just as much, or more, over Mark. That, more than anything else is what has kept me so isolated from others. I can't talk to my friends about how I feel because of the shame and, of course, there is always the guilt. I am so sure that if I reveal what has happened to our family, my friends will judge me. I wonder how you can accept his illness so easily."

"Of course, it's different being a parent," Paul said. "I knew it was really hard for you but I didn't take it all that seriously. I could separate myself from Mark and go on with my life pretty normally. Of course, it wasn't a topic I cared to discuss with my friends, either. When I didn't have him around, I would just as soon not think about him and I didn't."

If Paul was as detached as he would have me believe, I wondered how he could have shown as much consideration for his father and me as he did over those years. One time when we returned from a weekend away, I found a box of candy on the table.

There was a note that said, "I haven't done anything for you for a long time. Love, Paul."

For someone who didn't give Christmas or birthday presents, this was a gesture that was both surprising and appreciated. We needed all the affirmation we could get those days. I decided to tell Paul things that I had withheld in the past, partly to fill in for him things he did not know and also as a way to encourage him to get things off his chest. I was pretty sure he wasn't talking about personal things with his friends.

I went on, "I haven't told you how many times he called the hospital where Dad worked or came bursting into his offices. One time when he was brought into the emergency at the hospital, the psychiatrist who had an office next to Dad's treated him. Now he knew about our son. Mark often called the hospital collect demanding Dad. We were sure everyone in the hospital knew about it. We felt exposed and humiliated.

"He contaminated everything around us, our friends, our work relationships and home.

"He would show up at our church disoriented, sometimes in out-landish dress. Everyone would see our crazy son. It seemed that everyone we knew was pulled in and affected by him. Our privacy was outrageously violated."

I sensed Paul's annoyance and felt my chest tighten. I hoped fervently that we should be able to continue to talk and hear each other. I wondered how much of this review of the past Paul could tolerate. It was the first time we had ever talked together like this. Studying Paul's reaction, I sat quietly. When he spoke, he focused on his frustration and anger with his father.

"Dad didn't look at the situation at home very closely," he said. "All those years Mark was running his business from your house, when you complained Dad turned the other way. He never thought things were as serious as you made them out to be and would ignore your asking for him to support you."

I held my tongue and resisted the impulse to explain and defend Roy. Though I hadn't thought of going back into childhood memories, I realized that they were all part of what we were dealing with. Relationship difficulties began long before Mark's illness.

I told him that I planned to talk with his sisters, Beth and Deborah, as I was talking with him and that we would all, then, talk together as a family.

"You'll have further opportunity to say what you think and feel then, directly to each one of them," I said.

"Oh, if you get the three of us together, you can be sure Dad won't be in on it. He could never take it when there was too much conflict. I would look around for Dad when we were all together arguing or discussing some conflict and he would be gone, evaporated. He just didn't deal with a lot of things in the family," Paul retorted.

I recalled all the times that Roy and I arranged to hold family meetings to discuss family issues. We met with so much resistance from one or another of the children, over time we gave up. This was probably not the time to point this fact out to Paul.

"I know Dad wants to be involved and I do not think that he will 'evaporate' when the three of you are ready to sit down with us." I said.

Showing no signs of wanting to end our visit, Paul responded when I gently nudged him to talk about Mark's illness. Picking up the thread of an earlier conversation he said, "Well, of course, not only are you his parents, you both are counselors. It must have been pretty bad to have your clients see and know about your own crazy kid. I can see how that would have been tough for you, his showing up everywhere as he did. I was glad not to be home, I can tell you!"

"Besides feeling vulnerable professionally, we felt guilty and judging of ourselves after Mark broke down. I was sure that you and the other children judged us for the way we parented Mark," I said.

"No, I don't think you could have done anything different that would have helped. I think it was the way he was. I don't think parents have that much influence on their kids, how they turn out. I didn't and don't blame you for Mark. I saw you blaming each other but I didn't agree with that."

We talked about what Mark would have been like if we had been more strict or a different kind of parent. Focusing on the "if onlys", I heard myself saying things that Roy and I had said over and over to one another. I was groping, with Paul, to come to an understanding of what had happened to us. As if understanding would lesson the pain or make our situation more bearable.

Paul became annoyed. He said, "Oh, Mom, all that stuff you're saying. We just don't know. You take too much responsibility for him and I don't think you should. He was never easy for anyone to control. How could you have been harder on him? I can't imagine the kids blaming the parents."

For days Paul's words echoed in my head. "We just don't know. We just don't know."

I wondered what would be changed if we knew how and why Mark became ill. Why was I preoccupied with trying to get others to help me understand? Perhaps I would be more accepting of his fate and feel the pain less. I had memorized a number of poems of St. John of the Cross during dark days as a hedge against despair. I remembered a verse from one of them now. Words of the last verse of "I Came into the Unknown," flashed into my mind.

> And if you wish to hear the highest science leads to an ecstatic feeling of the most holy Being, and from his mercy comes his deed to let us stay unknowing, rising beyond all science.

Maybe it is not only unnecessary for us to understand some things but even merciful that we don't.

Why it was, I cannot say, but after our discussion and my recalling this poem, I lost my obsession with trying to understand. I felt a burden lifted, however slight.

"I asked you to come tonight because I want to include the perspective of the children in the book. Would you have a problem with that?" I asked.

"No, it doesn't matter to me. I have nothing to hide. I imagine it could be helpful to you to write a book from the perspective of the parent. You have gone through a lot since Mark went off the deep end. Yeah, I think writing a book is a pretty good idea. It could be interesting.

"One thing I noticed. You and Dad blamed each other a lot. I think it was misplaced in a lot of ways."

Paul's comment took me back to a time when Roy and I fought more than I care to remember. While both Paul and Mark were still home, Paul would witness most of our fighting, which was frequently over Mark who would be away. I seized the opportunity to recall that time now. Perhaps, as a young adult, years later, Paul could now talk with me about that time.

"Looking back now," I opened, "Dad and I did not realize what we were dealing with. We thought the kinds of problems we were having were somewhat normal. I knew that Mark had serious personality problems and was probably more aware than Dad because I saw much more of him and how he functioned. Dad dismissed my frustrations and assessment as exaggerated and my problem alone. We disagreed constantly about what to do about Mark's problems in which he involved us. Dad pleaded with me to give Mark more time."

"If we give him the time he needs, when he leaves, he'll leave for good and then we'll be really free," was the way he put it.

"I wanted to believe he was right and I put up with as much as I could stand. It was the constant tension around Mark that caused our fighting because as soon as Mark moved away, the fighting ceased. Life became pleasant for the two of us. I felt really guilty for your having to hear us and live with all our fighting during that period. I was sure that it influenced you to move out as early as you did. It hurt me that you never wanted to stay overnight once you left but could certainly understand why you wouldn't because Mark was a constant topic of discussion one way or another. The focus was always an Mark." I stopped to hear Paul's reaction.

"I really don't remember all that well," Paul confessed.

"About the fighting?" I asked incredulously.

"Well, not really," he replied.

What I had suffered regret and guilt over for years, Paul dismissed lightly.

Even if he remembered and was bothered more than he admitted, he did not have anything more to say just then.

After we took a break to stretch we talked for hours about the past. Paul told me how it was for him growing up in our family and I told him about how it was for me in mine. The mutual love and respect between us was apparent. I felt lucky.

"I've wandered many times if your reluctance to have children has something to do with Mark's illness, the mental illness in our family?" I asked.

"No, not really. I want kids. You looking for more grandchildren, Mom?" he laughed.

I didn't need to answer him. He already knew how much I cherished my grandmother role.

"I remembered when your Dad and I were planning to marry, I did not think it was fair to withhold information from him about my father though my father was dead, and I could have avoided the issue. When I told him about my father, he felt as you do, that it would not affect our lives or our children."

We were naive to think we could write off this illness so easily. Yet I am glad that Paul feels the same way, that you take your chances no matter what the circumstance. In addition, it is the human belief that "it could never happen to me."

Paul wanted to talk more about Mark and went on, "He always got jobs for which he had no skills then would say, 'Oh, I'll have to learn how to do that.' He never did things traditionally, learning and building a step at a time. He wanted to start at the top. He had so many wild schemes for himself, unrealistic."

I agreed, "He thought he could skip steps, take shortcuts and get to the same place as someone who had taken years to learn a skill. Maybe that had to do with his thinking process, which could have been faulty from very early. He hated being a beginner. Remember how impatient and angry he became when we were learning to water ski? He expected to take right off even though none of us could without practice."

"That's right! He never learned the concept of building on knowledge. He thought he was able to do things without lessons and if he couldn't, he would become angry and frustrated." Paul shifted in his chair, was quiet for a while then went on, "He never really learned to work the way most of us do. He manipulated his way out of work. He didn't get through that much school. High school isn't hard to get through. He never accomplished much during his college years, did he?" Apparently Paul knew no more than I of what Mark was accomplishing in college.

"I don't know how he did." I said. "He would never let me see his grades. I suspect he didn't always go to class when he said he did. Once he moved out, of course, I had no idea how he was doing in college classes. I was inclined to trust that he was going to school if he said he was. I believed him more than he deserved, I fear."

Paul seemed at a loss to say anything more so I asked him another question.

"Did you ever feel scared? Sometimes he was so violent around here, screaming, throwing and breaking things. Dad and I were scared sometimes."

Paul leaned back in his chair and yawned. It was getting late. He looked at his watch, "No, I didn't." Then, apologetically, "I'm sorry, but the answer is no. I didn't feel afraid. I knew him all my life. I suppose I was confident that I could handle him. I am bigger than he is."

I laughed, relieved that Paul's experience was less difficult than I had pictured. He went on.

"Not scared. Frustrated. That's the word. Mark was very frustrating person to live with. You always knew if you left him alone, he was going to do something dumb. Like forget his key and then crawl in a window and leave it open to the street all night. You couldn't trust him. Especially after his illness. You just couldn't trust him. There was always the hope that 'Mark's going to get better.' He was always crazy. It was only that before his breakdown, he was less crazy. When he was running his paint company he was totally crazy. The only reason I could tolerate it was that he was out of my way. He was always hoping that someday he would get himself organized.

"When I look back, from junior high and high school- I can't say before that—I think he was totally crazy. And after he had his painting business, well, in that business a responsible guy is one in a thousand. That's the only reason he could make it work as long as he did. People like Jim, (our daughter, Beth's brother-in-law) in the building and contracting business, are rare. They aren't usually that honest and responsible.

"Mark was lucky in that he had some responsible guys working for him. That's probably why it worked. He was so frustrating to me all those years. I am amazed you put up with him as long as you did."

Though it was getting late, Paul made no move to leave. At this first opportunity to talk about the years of frustrations he had experienced growing up with his difficult brother, he showed no signs of running out of things to say. Even as we shared, I was painfully aware of how much of our time and energy had been poured into Mark at the sacrifice of the other children. While I felt the pain, I knew that it could have been no different. I was glad that it was not too late to re-establish relations with these three other children, now as adults.

I felt a keen drop in my energy, suddenly. I noticed that I was unable to assimilate or hear any more of Paul's negative feelings even though he seemed to be far from finished expressing them. He began yawning continuously reminding me that he had worked a long day before he arrived at the house.

"Why don't we call it quits for tonight?" I suggested. "I will review and write up our conversation and then after you look it over, I would like you to come over and talk again."

"Sounds good," he said. He got up, hugged me and left with a "Good night, Mom," as he closed the door.

Tired but exhilarated, I put away my materials and went up to bed, glad that I was alone for the week-end to process and think about all the things Paul and I had talked about.

My exhilaration did not last. The next morning I was shrouded in gloom. My mind could only remember the negative things I had heard Paul say. They rattled in my head as accusations and judgments compounding the never-ending guilt I felt over my faulty parenting and the fate of our son. It was a few days before I was ready to listen to the tapes of our conversation. By then I was able to appreciate how valuable our conversation had been for us both.

When Paul returned for the second time to talk, he had read what I had written. He had more things to say, I could tell.

First I asked, "Did I represent you fairly?"

"It's okay. I said it that way. That's what I said," he answered.

"Good, shall we start?" I asked even before he could answer I said, "You said when I asked you how you felt when you thought about Mark, 'I don't think about him. That's it! I don't think about him. I feel too bad so I don't think about him, period.'"

"That's true, I don't think about him," Paul said as he squirmed in his chair, apparently uncomfortable.

I persisted, "But when you do think about him you feel bad?"

"Yeah," quietly.

I felt I must tread lightly to keep Paul talking for I know he was having some feeling about talking more about what he had successfully avoided to now.

"Can you say more about that?" I asked softly.

"Well, you know, there's something to get sad about. Missing Mark. He was part of the family for a long time. It's like there's a hole in the family now. It's like when we get together, there's that hole. It never seems quite complete when we have Thanksgiving dinner. Like you said, last Thanksgiving, 'This is the family!' It doesn't seem like the family without Mark."

"That's interesting. At our other meeting you focused a lot on how horrible it was being a kid in this family," I said.

"Hey, Mom, you've got it wrong. I didn't say how bad it was. I just said how irresponsible Mark was and how chaotic things were. He was a flake."

Since I did not need him to expand on what he meant by flake, I changed the subject.

"One other thing. Do you worry about mental illness cropping up for you if you have a family? I know we talked briefly about this once but I would like to hear you say more about that."

"Well, I don't ever think about it. I expect life to turn out. It would be a really bad attitude to come from, expecting mental illness. Though, of course there is a strain in our family, and it comes through you, little mother. Nope, I don't think about it in relation to me. It isn't even a remote consideration for me."

I knew that I had come a long way in learning to accept the illness that was in my childhood family. When Paul, lightly but truthfully, pointed his finger at me as the culprit, the carrier of mental illness, I heard him without so much as a blink of the eye or even the tiniest flicker in my stomach. Roy, who was in the room, flinched.

He was surprised when I told him later that I no longer blame myself or anyone that Paul's remark proved how far I've come when I did not have the slightest negative reaction.

"Our life isn't over yet, Roy. We don't know what illness or grief may come through you or any one of us. Like Paul says, 'we take what comes.'"

I am glad, and hope it is true, that Paul has no fear for his own stability nor that this mental illness gene will come out in his family. He is secure within himself.

He has always demonstrated his ability to handle life. He worked hard through college and enjoys a successful career as a professional. He knows how to balance work and play. He has many friends, myriad interests. When he was growing up, I watched him with pride as he matured and moved from one stage to another.

Paul's current fears are centered around the future with Mark. Roy joined us as we discussed Mark's condition. Though I assured Paul that Mark has deteriorated in the last three years so that I have my doubts that he shall ever get out of the hospital, he would not be convinced. Because of what we went through for so many years, none of us wants Mark back in our lives anymore, not if he weren't drastically changed. My educated guess is that this cannot happen.

Paul argued, "Well, you know with Mark. He can change so quickly. He could just make a complete turn around, get out of the hospital and start the chaos all over."

"I know that is your persistent prediction and fear but I want to assure you I do not share your opinion. I saw him last week. He is deteriorating so rapidly and severely that his doctor agrees with my prediction that he will never recover." I said.

Paul does not readily or easily change his opinion on a subject. I wondered if he heard what I had said.

He insisted, "You forget how many times Mark has gotten out of the hospital in the past, Mom. He could change just like that. If you will recall, it is only recently that he talked about getting out when you went to see him."

It sounds like Paul worries that Mark will get out and no effort on my part would reassure him differently. He was right, recently there was a period when Mark made a surprising spontaneous recovery, which prompted the staff to talk about release. We all felt nervous then. The change was of such brief duration, we realized, as we had suspected from past experience, that the staff had been hasty in assuming his condition would last. After that episode, Mark deteriorated drastically. Paul refused to be reassured.

Maybe it is unacceptable to Paul that Mark's fate should lay in our dire prediction. He could be afraid to hope that his frustrations with Mark are over. I chose to let the matter rest. We would only get into a fruitless argument over who was right or wrong. In this case neither of us wants to be right. He does not want Mark to come out causing chaos in our lives and I do not want Mark to be hopelessly ill.

As Roy, Paul and I talked late into the evening, I felt and saw the barriers to our communication dissolving. None of us needed to become defensive when someone or the other expressed a truth that jarred us. Paul expressed warm appreciation for his father and me. But more important to my mother-heart was his willingness to confess his love for his brother, which could only happen once the resentments were cleared away. That went further to heal the wound in me than anything else that had occurred between us. Love is a powerful healer. I have faith that there is enough in all of us in our family to heal us all.

Chapter IX.

I flew to Colorado in 1987 to spend a week with our second daughter, Deborah. She is now a practicing child psychologist, wife and mother of three, Matthew 15, Sarah 12, and Sam 6. Because the children have been the lure that brings me to Colorado often, I had to take to heart the daughters', Beth and Deborah, accusation that I hardly noticed them or spent time with them since they have had children. It was not that I loved my daughters less but that I loved being with their children so much that there didn't seem enough time for them. This time my intent was to have a separate time and interview with Deborah.

We arranged for her husband to mind the children while we went out to a quiet restaurant for dinner where we could converse uninterrupted.

I turned on the tape recorder, and opened our conversation, "I want you to begin telling me about how it was for you when your brother broke down, starting from those early memories. Can you remember?"

"Yes, I remember it. I had to rely on what you told me. You were coming out for a conference and ski trip and I thought when I got your call, 'something with Mark. Always something with Mark,'" She paused, stared at the candles, her brow furrowed. "You and Dad were so upset when you came it was hard to make any sense out of it. I was concerned for you more than for Mark as it was so new and we didn't have any idea where it would go or how bad it would get.

"My feelings were contaminated by my feelings for myself. You were coming to the mountains to be with me. I saw so little of you since I had gone away to college and then came here to graduate school. The whole time was spent with your having to call home to make some arrangements around Mark, and then your emotional involvement cheated me of you."

I had known how cheated she had felt and remembered that time with regret. How well I remembered. We were desperate to have Mark transferred to the University Hospital but could not arrange it before we left for our trip. We were fearful that if we did not intervene he would be sent to the State Hospital and then we would have little or no say in his treatment. At that time, of course, we would not have been ready to let him go to his fate, which we were confident we could influence for his good.

"I felt ambivalent," Deborah went on, "I wanted to hear yet, when we talked about it, it was so upsetting to you that it spoiled our time together. Another thing that was hard was that it was my field of study. I was trying to make sense out of it and yet, being at a distance, it was hard to know what was going on. While it was a relief being so far away, it also left me out of so much. I confess that I was glad to be spared the day-to-day involvement. It certainly made it easier for me to go on with my life normally."

"Over the years, did you begin to see what was going on?" I asked.

"It took a long time with Mark to see what kind of response there was going to be with all the drug treatment he was given. I felt a lot of frustration because at the beginning we didn't get enough sense of what was happening to know how to proceed with his treatment. I was frustrated with the difficulty of diagnosis and would get pulled in at an intellectual level to try to understand. After awhile I realized that his was a very difficult case, that it wasn't clear cut nor easily diagnosed. I wrote a letter to one of the doctors at Langely Porter to get some information. The way I coped with my emotions was to try to figure it out on a professional level. That way I could handle the feelings more easily."

What feelings did she have toward her brother? She spoke with so little that I wondered if she had any. Maybe Mark's illness had not affected her as much as I had imagined. I told her now how I had felt when my brother was seriously injured.

"When my brother had his accident, the year he fell off the ladder, you remember, and he was disabled for the rest of his life, I did not grieve a lot for him. I suppose because he was old and had already lived most of his life. Also, we were so far apart and had not seen each other very often for years. It was not anything like having something happen to a child, one so young as Mark. I wonder what you can say to that." I invited her to speak.

She did not respond directly but began discussing her other brother, Paul.

"Paul, I think, got the brunt of it because he was at home but not having his own family like Beth. I was so far away, I didn't bear much of the day-to-day stress you all endured. Even though I often heard what happened, it was already over and I had not gone through the trauma with you." She looked down at her plate and then again at me. Her face was soft in the candlelight, which cast a shadow across her pretty face.

"The thing that horrified me was that Mark would go into Dad's office and create all sorts of chaos. When I heard that, I would be mortified and totally humiliated for you both. You and Dad had to deal with all the guilt issues, the worry of 'if I had done this or that' plus the attachment and all the responsibility of handling everything that came along, one crisis after another."

I was reminded, as she talked, of the humiliating hours I stood in line at the welfare office to get Mark on disability when it became apparent that he would not be able to work or assume responsibility financially for his care. After his business was settled, there was little left for medical care.

We were clear that it would be impossible for us to assume responsibility for his bills.

Deborah went on, "I just felt sad for Mark. But it's real different when you're a sibling and especially since I don't think any of us ever felt that close to him. He was hard to connect with, so it wasn't like I had lost a soul mate. Looking back and thinking it over now, I think his troubles began as far back as high school. He could not make friends with girls even though he wanted very badly to do so."

"Yes," I agreed. "By high school I was worried. He was so out of touch with his feelings and the feelings of others. I hoped that he would grow out of it but at the same time I worried. Then he had so many schemes and plans, though they could be exciting, sometimes they were unrealistic and he couldn't see it. I think it was his enthusiasm that we caught and enjoyed."

"Right." Deborah said. "It was easy to say that he was our eccentric creative member, and, in some ways, he was if he had been more together."

"That was what fooled Dad and me, kept us from seeing more clearly how Mark was developing."

As our sensitive child, Deborah caught my self-criticism. She would not let me get by with it.

"Mom, it didn't fool you that much. You had him in therapy when he was a kid. You worried about him a lot, and now we see it was for good reason. You tried to get us all into family therapy when we were teen-agers and he, the one you were most concerned about, would resist the most. You didn't want him to be singled out as the one with the problems, rather wanting each of us to assume responsibility for what went on among us in the family so that we couldn't blame everything on Mark. I remember your frustration with trying to discipline him."

Her voice was soft and low. She was remembering other incidents. As if she were right in the scene, she related incident after incident, "the time he broke the table, then the time he crawled out the window when you sent him to his room to punish him, and the time he took your car and wrecked it." The memories flooded into our heads as we looked at one another across the table. We stopped talking only when the waiter came to our table. Though the material we were discussing brought me fresh pain, the shared intimacy was something I had missed since Deborah had left home. When the waiter left, Deborah continued.

"When I was in high school and college, I used to think that you and Dad should exercise better control over Mark. If you would do something different, then Mark would be different. It's like you expect your parents to fix everything. I would think you should have been able to control him. Now I have so much better appreciation of how difficult he was to manage. I used to wish he wouldn't eat with us. He spilled things, knocked stuff over, took more than his share and always caused some commotion at the dinner table. He had to eat alone at the breadboard so much. You know, like Pigpen always has a cloud of dust around him. He was like that, stirring things up."

"He always kept the pot boiling was the way Dad and I expressed it." I said.

"If I had lived close to him over these last years, I would have had a hard time with getting sucked in; though I admit I feel guilty being so far and not bearing the burden with you, like I was getting off scot-free."

We shifted to talk of the years of Mark's growing up. "Probably because Mark had you as parents, he was not especially violent when he went off the deep end. If you had tried to control him in a harsh way, he would have had more aggression," Deborah commented.

Deborah confirmed what I had often thought myself. When Mark was severely distraught during his most violent outbursts, even when he was utterly desperate, he always stopped himself short of hurting anyone. Painful though our lives have been, I have been grateful that he did not cause additional heartache and pain to us or to other families by acts of violence.

I answered, "Well, we really don't know, do we? In any event it gives us comfort to know it could have been worse."

Deborah had been complimenting us, her parents, and I had brushed it off. It was hard for me to feel I had done anything right with Mark. Still I felt her approval.

When she looked down, her hair fell across her face and her voice was soft," When I was a little kid, I used to worry that I would have a brother in jail. There was something so intense and negative about him. We were upset one time when Beth said to me, I wish he would die."

This seemed a good time to share with Deborah about a neighbor's dire prediction, something I had not told anyone.

"I've never told anyone this before," I began. "It's so far out, I'm a bit embarrassed to tell you. You recall Mrs. S. who was the fussy neighbor, the one who would call the police on slight provocation. If a ball would go into her yard, it was a major catastrophe for her. She was a rather negative woman. Though we asked her to bring her complaints to us to settle, she would not do that but would call the police. When they came they, too, preferred that we settle our neighborhood disputes among ourselves. Things that bugged her were usually simple ones, like the kids running across her yard.

"She told me one time that Mark would 'end up in jail.' Remembering the fairy tale where the curse was removed by a good fairy, I often wished there were a good fairy who would intervene for us and remove the curse. Thus far we have not come across anyone who has given us hope that if some conditions are met, that Mark will recover."

Deborah smiled. "Not bad, Mom. Kinda Jungian, psychological, huh?" She went on with her thoughts. "It's so sad. He's just such a sad kid. It's really a tragedy for him. You know the biggest thing for me was gratitude that I had some distance and then a lot of worry about you and Dad, what it was doing to your lives and feeling really bad about that. He demanded so much, took so much as a child, and you never got anything back for all you invested.

"Then, as an adult, he takes your friends and contaminates and poisons your relationships. Like the time he told the neighbor couple that you said they weren't very friendly, and they haven't spoken to you since. And the other couple that walks by your house and won't speak. There are also the couples that had been longtime friends that couldn't take Mark so they stopped seeing you. That was so hard for you to lose so many friends, diminishing your support system to a trickle. And it wasn't just the close relationships, it was every orbit, polluting and poisoning the environment with his outrageous behavior and manipulation. Not only did he drain your energy but also he took away from you what you had built up with so much hard work, robbing you of the professional respect you had earned…a wasted life, a sad thing for us all.

"Even as I was worried about you, I felt some responsibility to stay in touch with Mark, to let him know that I cared. However, any contact I did have with him would feel really yucky. Like he would call me at four in the morning and he would be so off the wall. Then Jim said I would be upset for a long time after the contact. While I wanted to stay in touch, I was relieved when I didn't hear from him for long periods of time.

"Remember when I was in high school? He admired me so much. We had some good talks. We had some fun together camping, talking about literature and when he went to the University I took an interest in his courses. Then one day he turned on me completely. He did not want to hear my name mentioned. It didn't make sense, I had done nothing to him. I was doing my work at school and succeeding. Ah, maybe that was it. He was beginning to fail. Well, anyhow when he would call me and I would wake from a sound sleep at three in the morning, he would want to read me a whole chapter from D.H. Lawrence and want to discuss it. A kid who couldn't get his shoes on the right foot, was not managing his next meal wanted to make connection with me on an intellectual level. It was as if that was a way he thought he could connect with me, and he was desperate to make a connection to someone. Gosh, it was sad, really sad. How do you make sense out of it? I couldn't."

I understood so perfectly what Deborah was saying that there hardly seemed to be anything to add. I picked up a thread of our conversation and went on.

"I always felt I should stay in contact and be available to Mark when he needed me, yet it was so distressing when we did connect that eventually, to protect myself emotionally, I did not initiate contact and hoped he would leave us alone. When we decided to get an unlisted phone so that he could not phone us, I said to my doctor, 'What if something happened and he couldn't reach me?' We both laughed. Something was always happening and he seemed to get out of trouble or find someone to help him and eventually always reached us somehow. The decision to get an unlisted number supported my determination to protect and take care of myself."

We talked of the present situation where Mark was hospitalized and getting care.

I told Deborah, as I had told staff and doctors, how grateful I am that Mark is being cared for humanely. We spoke of the hopelessness of his case and the slim chance that he should ever recover.

"For the first four or five years, I used to think there might be something that would work. Now I have no trouble wishing he would die and be out of his misery. I really don't have a problem with wishing that, Mom." Deborah assured me.

"I'll tell you another fantasy I have had," I said. "Off and on I would and do wonder if Dad and I would give up all our private life, give up working and devote our time to Mark that he might have a chance. I was impressed by the couple that had an autistic child to whom they devoted every waking moment. The child recovered to become a normal child by four. I have had a persistent nagging thought that if enough sacrifice was made and enough prayers offered that Mark would be saved. I think it goes back to being that kid who thought she could help save her father if she only could get him out of bed in the morning. Who thought if she cared enough, he would get well. I wanted desperately for Mark to have another chance. Then I would remember that we had given all we had to give and done for him everything we knew how to do for twenty-one years and I would come back to reality. Your Dad was a good source of a reality check for me, too. I would ask myself, 'How long does one do for another? What good does it do if that other isn't capable of doing for himself?' All these questions keep re-occurring. There is no once and for all answer."

"Amen", Deborah said. "Right! You know, I think it's such a trap with someone like Mark who was so severely ill. You look at it so rationally, like if he did this or that or if he were motivated." Her voice rose as her agitation mounted. "It just can't happen for him! It just can't! I just hope that he...." She was quiet then repeated emphatically, I just hope that he..." again she hesitated and I said it for her "dies," I said.

"Yes, well...." That wish was fraught with more emotion than she had admitted earlier, perhaps more than she realized. She did not want to pursue it but went on hurriedly, "Remember in high school he would have these accidents?" She was angry. She hated when she cried, as if it were a sign of weakness. Was her anger to cover her tears? Her voice broke. "He ran into brick walls, rode his motorcycle dangerously, always on the edge. He had so little self-awareness. He was always a kind of spooky kid. Nothing ever anchors in him, it doesn't get through."

I agreed, "For sure. He was in restraints throughout the month of December. By March, following shock treatment, he seemed so normal that the staff was talking about releasing him to a halfway house. He called me, excited about what he was going to do when he was released. There seemed to be no awareness that he was a very sick person and that he would have to put taking care of himself first if he were going to stay out of the hospital. There's that total lack of awareness that you speak of that has always been there. It seems that it is impossible for this kind of person to deal with the inner world. Is it the illness or is it him? I don't know. What I do know is that he won't last a month on the outside given his attitude. As it turns out, he was severely psychotic following that last lucid period. Thank God, he is not being released at this time."

Deborah repeated, "Nothing gets integrated. It doesn't get anchored and he seems unable to benefit from experience. Nothing ever anchors!"

We both began talking at once, our thoughts mingling so that we spoke over one another. We were saying, in effect, "Yeah, yeah, yeah! That's the way I saw it, too." These were wonderful moments. I felt understood as well as exonerated. If all we were saying were true, I could stop blaming myself. What a joy to be with my brilliant daughter who had always been an anchoring person in my life, her love of life, her bright mind, her sweetness with children…I like everything about her.

When we turned off the recorder to make some decisions with our waiter we took some time to enjoy our dinner and each other. Then Deborah began in a new vein.

"Mom you know you have said that, if you hadn't had a son like that, it would have been different for you, you might have had a satisfying career after we were grown. Well, I think at first part of my reaction to Mark's stuff was my own need to break away from my family and work through my beliefs around what you might have done differently as parents. Now I have a whole different sense of it…like, you know, he brought a whole lot of negative weird stuff. It profoundly influenced the interactions in our family.

I looked at her appreciatively, "Like perhaps Dad and I wouldn't have fought so much normally. You mean things like that?"

"Yes," she said. "I always knew you loved each other but the fighting was hard to take. I guess when I came to marriage, I had few illusions about it being living happily ever after, and I certainly have learned how to fight." Then proudly, "I have probably taught Jim a thing or two about how to fight.

"Another thing about Mark is that he needs a setting that is highly structured and contained. That's probably why he didn't break down until he moved out and you no longer took care of him. Maybe some parents can have their ill members at home. They are more manageable than

Mark. He needs to be in a hospital," spoken emphatically and with feeling. "He needs to be where he is."

This was not only an experienced professional. This was a sister of a mentally ill person talking about her experience as a sister, a child growing up with this brother.

It was hard for Deborah to give Mark any credit on the positive side. When I mentioned an incident where Mark was delightful she looked puzzled.

"Delightful?" she asked.

When I spoke of how bright he was, she did not respond. Does she have too much resentment blocking her ability to see Mark complete or am I blinded? I imagine both. Who of us sees it all? Scripture says, "Now we see in a glass darkly" and that someday we shall see things as they really are. I certainly identify with the first part of that statement, that we "see in a glass darkly." That is what makes us human, our limited perceptions and abilities. Maybe someday or somewhere we will have a more complete understanding of things.

I began to feel defensive for Mark. I wanted to say, "he wasn't all bad." He must have tried or had a terrible time with his inability to make and keep relationships. For a time I found myself unable to remain objective and keep my perspective clear. My maternal protective instincts were aroused. Deborah, now a parent, could understand.

We discussed how bitter I felt for a while and wondered why my children would want to have children given the history of my family. Though Deborah argues that statistics are on her side she did confess, "Well, it goes through my head when I have real difficult times with Matthew. I worry a little. Do you worry about Matthew?"

Not wanting to empower such a fearful thought, I would have preferred not to talk about it but it was out in the open now. I was tempted to dismiss the idea.

That would have been deceitful and Deborah would have known anyhow. I would try to soften what I had to say. I thought how to word my response. She looked at me, "Well, do you?" she said.

"After his difficult birth, when he was so jumpy and sleeping little, I wondered about him. As he has developed, I see so much of our Mark in him, the intensity and the curiosity. With his maturation, I have been able to dismiss my thoughts as groundless worries and committing them to God, to let be. I feel somewhat secure in the knowledge that what we expect to happen isn't usually the thing that does. In my most wild fantasies, I would not have expected Mark to become as ill as he has." As I talked I avoided using the word, "schizophrenia." I hate the word. It is so damning and final. Just saying the word makes me feel upset and I would never say it in the same breath with which I spoke the name of my grandson. I reminded myself that our thoughts could not take wing and become reality. Still I felt uncomfortable voicing such concerns for our first grandson.

Pushing her plate away from her, Deborah looked up at me. Her voice was cool, matter of fact as she recited some statistics to me. "Well, you would never refrain from having a kid, taking a chance if you want kids." Then confidently she said, "As a sibling of a schizophrenic I stand a 2% chance of having the illness repeat itself. That is no higher than the chances in the population at large. I'm not so concerned as I am two generations removed from your father and both you and Dad have been stable and strong.

Returning to the subject of her brother, we reviewed more of the past. We recalled one incident after another in Mark's childhood that coalesced to form a picture of a boy having more than normal growing up problems. Deborah said, "Remember when we went water skiing? If you didn't bring him in just right, he would fall apart and he would make such a scene we would all be miserable."

My memory was jogged around similar incidents when we were with friends, "And embarrassed," I added.

Then Deborah said, "Mark just had this real absent quality as if he had no awareness of what was going on around him."

I was amazed at how much Deborah had seen and wondered about as she was growing up, things she had never voiced. She had always been a keen observer of people and relationships. When I was holding women's' support groups in our home, she confessed to me years later that she had sat on the stairs and listened. When Roy and I were having a silent disagreement she would generally pick up that something was wrong.

She would say, "You're mad at Dad, aren't you?"

More to relieve the tension than that we were finished, we spoke of matters with the children, our friends and her friends and career plans that she and Jim were making. Deborah brought us back.

"The other thing I felt bad about was when he was showing up at your friends. You had nowhere that you could get away from him. He took so much out of everyone and yet his is like a wasted life. There's nothing to show for it."

In the past I might have waxed philosophically or theologically but by this time I was more than inclined to agree that his was a wasted life. I could see nothing good that had come out of it or out of his illness. Maybe all things do not work together for good for those who love God or I don't know what that means.

Deborah signed wistfully. "I wonder what our family would have been like if we hadn't had Mark."

Her remark prompted us to indulge our fantasies that included "living happily ever after," with no tragedy. For twenty minutes we discussed pleasant possibilities, things we wished had happened, instead of what did. We agreed finally as Deborah remarked, "It surely would have been different."

Beginning to feel talked out as well as listened out, I said, "Is there anything more you want to say?"

She spoke of the same things Paul had said about low frustration tolerance and began repeating what we had gone over so many times, like how he walked around the house during puberty with an erect penis sticking out of his pajamas and his lack of awareness of what he was doing.

"He's like a little chaos producer." Deborah added.

"What chaos did he produce for you? Have you suffered so much?" I asked. As if that needed elaboration. Perhaps we were both getting tired and running out of things to say.

"Oh, Mom, he made it hard in your marriage and…"

"He didn't succeed in ruining life for any of us, right?" I said. I wanted to hear something positive about Mark. I wanted to defend him.

"Right." She did not argue the point. Neither of us wanted to argue or spoil our evening. That happened far too often. We would be dealing with something with Mark and soon Mark would be forgotten and we would be arguing.

Still it was not right to blame Mark for all the unhappiness we had suffered, making him a scapegoat. Roy and I fought hard against that when we were raising the children, for we saw it happening. We were sometimes guilty ourselves of assuming Mark was at fault when something went wrong without investigating as we might. If I were now free of blaming, I should not have reacted to Deborah's remark. I was not free. I could still feel the sting of blame and criticism, my own, of myself.

When I realized how ill our son was, I had no blame for what he had done or for the trouble he had caused. Though I wished it could have been different, I know Mark wished the same. Mark, like my father, was the victim of an illness that affected his ability to control himself or to make wise and rational judgments.

Deborah spoke softly, "I know a lot of families with problems like yours. I hear so many stories with the same theme. I think you have done really well. Given what Mark presented, I think you did an amazing job of trying to parent him."

Her words fell like a benediction on my ears. I had heard very little praise for my efforts, the least from myself. Now, as a parent herself, Deborah does not judge us as harshly as she might have when she first began her practice as a psychologist. She has come to an appreciation of what a challenge it is to be a parent.

We relived the fear that Mark would intrude upon Deborah's wedding. She said," He intruded upon so many parties those years, causing so much chaos. I thought I couldn't bear it if he showed up at my wedding."

Though the temperature had not changed in the room, my teeth were chattering. I began to shiver uncontrollably. Could it be that while I thought I was feeling only calm and objective most of the time, that on another level, I was feeling something else? I could hardly bear to hear or talk about another incident of those years. I was grateful that Deborah sensed my need and began talking about my brothers and sisters, a subject easier to talk about. We very soon agreed to end our conversation and go back to the children and home.

Our talk provided the outlet I needed for my continuing agony and anxiety. Deborah, too, seemed freer that week. Though we did not consciously avoid talking about Mark, now that we had talked openly and at length, neither of us seemed to have a need to discuss him. It afforded me welcome relief.

Chapter X.

Beth, our oldest daughter responded favorably when I asked if she would talk to me about Mark. I went to her home where she lives with her husband and two children. She was neatly dressed in jeans and a shirt. Her long dark hair was pulled back off her pretty face. When I walked in her bright smile greeted me. With the children at school, she wanted to begin almost as soon as I arrived in order to take advantage of our time alone. This would be the first time in many years that she and I would talk intimately. With a catch in her voice she opened the conversation at once.

"This is the first time since Mark's breakdown that I have had a chance to talk with you about how I feel. I think you have been concerned about me a few times but basically it has been a really hard thing for you and Dad to talk about. I remember being frustrated trying to talk with you, especially Dad, he couldn't be at all objective. My outlet was to talk freely with friends."

I cringed as I pictured the many friends that she had told about our son. Seeing my reaction, Beth asked me what she had said.

"It's nothing that you said. It's just that I feel so ashamed. I don't want others to know about Mark. I still want to hide and go on as if everything is fine in our family," I said.

Though I had not meant to be critical, Beth was defensive when she said, "Mom, I had to talk to someone. I had to do something about the anger and frustration I felt at being cut off from talking with you about Mark. Only my friends seemed to have open ears. Besides, I never felt shame about my brother and his behavior. I never felt his actions were a reflection on me or a result of something I did. Of course, understandably, you as a parent would feel guilt and shame. I never did. For a long time I know it was a stigma for you and Dad, not for me." She was crying.

"I got my release talking about it to other people. One thing I learned from this is that there are no guarantees in raising your kids. Even though I once believed parents to be responsible for their children's personality disorders, I now feel otherwise. Too many factors (peers, heredity, environment, siblings, culture) interact to mold a person's character and view of himself. Of course, parents play a significant role in shaping their child's self-esteem and view of the world, especially in some cases of child abuse. There are parents, and I see mine as part of this group, that provide a stable and fairly normal home and still the child deviates from the norm and becomes a disruptive member of society.

"You can do your best and you don't know what's going to happen. Even if you knew about his condition, you wouldn't know what to do about it to change it.

"I used to think that Dad was not disciplined enough with Mark, that he used to let Mark get by with murder. Mark was always manipulating. I thought he should have had greater consequences for things that he did. Now I think that if he had been stricter maybe Mark would be in jail or dead today."

As Beth poured out her well formulated thoughts, I realized that, though I could not have listened before now, she, too, would not have been ready until now, to articulate her thoughts and feelings. What she had learned could have come out only after years of struggle.

"Are you saying that you don't feel as judging of Dad as you did?" I asked as I recalled the many times she had complained about her father to me.

She hesitated, searching for the right words, "Well, ah, yes, I was judging of Dad and, at the same time, I don't think a change in Dad's behavior would change what has happened to Mark. It is like Mark was born with a birth defect.

"Remember when I went to that TV show and asked the psychic about Mark? I phrased the question so that she wouldn't know if his problem was physical or mental. She said he would recover. I had such high hopes but over time I found that hope was more painful to live with than to accept him as he is. I have now given up hope for his recovery and accept that this is his life. If he gets better that would be wonderful. Though I think it's over for him. That is more of a tragedy and harder to accept than if you have the condition from birth where you have no expectations on the child. Born blind or deaf, parents know what they have to deal with. Instead, you raise a child normally and all of a sudden this happens and you think he can be cured because he was so normal. It is really hard to believe that he is incurable, yet I have come to that conclusion."

She was thoughtful as she said, "I wonder if there is some imbalance in him that, at this point in our technology, we do not know how to correct."

Suddenly, without warning, her anger erupted in sharp criticism of the psychiatric community for their inability to make a diagnosis.

"When Mark first had his problems you went to so much effort to get him into the right treatment program. You spent a lot of time and money. Then he made up his own mind when he lost out in the fine program you had him in down in Los Angeles. It was from there that he got into the State System."

Her anger vented, Beth's face relaxed. She sighed and went on. It was clear that she had a lot to say.

The more we talked the closer I felt to my daughter. We filled in spaces for each other where before there had been blanks. Our daughter had grown in understanding. While she did not see it herself, I could tell that she had come through well. While she resented us for not being there for her, at the same time, she did not realize how much she had been thrown back on her own resources and had not been found wanting. Through these years she took care of her children, maintained her home with artistry and charm for her family and created an atmosphere of love and acceptance for her husband's parents and her own. Even as I hurt, I basked in pride in my eldest child.

At times we turned off the recorder to hold each other and cry together. There is wisdom in the instruction to 'bear one another's burdens'. I felt the burden of the years lighten. Where I had expected to be criticized and judged by my children, I had found only a communication that revealed what sensitive young adults our three children had become.

"There was another show, "The Promise," that helped me see what it was like for Mark. I just hope that this life of his is going to mean something." Beth said.

"Mean something, like help someone else?" I asked.

"Oh, no, I wasn't thinking that so much as "she laughed self-consciously, "maybe put him on a different level in the hereafter because he suffered so much here." We laughed together. I was especially amused for this was my agnostic daughter talking about the hereafter. She added, "He's gone through so much shit here that he is going to be at a higher level than I'm going to be when I die. I'm glad we can talk about it now, Mom." Beth smiled.

"I am too. Maybe all this writing will facilitate the healing for me and the talks we are having be helpful to you. If nothing else, it has been very special having these individual talks with each of you," I said.

Beth said, "I think your Dad being sick made it real hard on you. And it's hard on Daddy, too. I didn't even think about it in regard to the profession, what a black eye that is, a slap in the face. But for you, having a father and then your own son, too. It was more than a slap in the face for you. It was real tough!

"When we were growing up you always wanted to stay on top of the depression. I know now that is the reason you went to groups and retreats to work on the emotional problems and your spiritual life—like you had to keep on top of the illness that might be dormant in you because of your family history. You had such a fear that the same thing might happen to you." She was crying as she reached out to hug me. "To have conquered that makes me very proud of you, by the way." Then sobbing unashamedly, she stammered, "but to have to see your son go the same way!"

For the first time, in years, I felt completely vindicated and understood. I had no idea that Beth had observed so much. She was a quiet child, engrossed in art projects all of her growing years. At one period in her life she hardly spoke but went directly to her room when she came home from school. All the drawings she made of little people were without mouths. I used to wonder, and even worry a little, about what those mouthless people represented for her. Were the little figures herself? Was she mute because she was seeing more than she could understand or articulate? Perhaps she did not confide in me because I was absorbed in myself and failed to hear her. Well, she was talking now.

Taken by surprise at her sympathy for me, I brushed away my own tears. I struggled, it is true, for years to keep on top of depression. I had worked hard, not only on my marriage and family but I was struggling for my life all those years.

Still crying, Beth continued, "I've had a lot of anger towards Mark growing up. He was always hard for me to get along with. I hated his manipulation of you and Dad. After his illness it got worse. He had you and Dad even more under his power than before. You couldn't enjoy your trips. Well, you couldn't enjoy anything. Present or not, he was always there with you."

"You're right on," I said. "It spilled over into our entire life. No matter what we did or where we went, there was always the memory and pain of our son."

"Well, he's not controlling you so much now. You're starting to let him go," she said.

"You know the story of the lost sheep in the Bible. If the shepherd loses one of his hundred, he leaves the ninety-nine and applies himself completely to finding the lost sheep. I think that's what parents do, too," I told her.

"I know," she said. "Andrew (her husband) likens your situation to that of the Prodigal Son. It is easy for him because he's not your child. Children see it differently. When you put all that energy into the one, the others get jealous. We felt that you were not grateful that we were doing well. It seemed like you had no time for us for years. When you were with us, you were really thinking about Mark. Often, when we were together, you had to handle something immediately. I felt, at times, that I had lost my mother and father. I used to feel pretty ripped off.

"But, back to the manipulation. I used to get so mad at Mark that one time I told him I wished something terrible would happen to him, like his wife, if he ever got married would divorce him! At that time that sounded like something really bad," she laughed. "Now something far worse than I wished on him did happen and I realize you have to be careful what you wish for because it may come true. Though I don't believe I made it happen or that I really feel guilty, yet it has crossed my thoughts at different times.

"Since I never had a close relationship with Mark, the illness touched me more in that I was angry with him for continuing to manipulate my Mom and Dad. Now I have lost all that anger and feel only pity and sadness for his life. I understand that he lacks control and can't see what he's doing.

"Prior to the onset of his illness, the stress was really bad between you and Dad and you called me a lot. One time you talked about moving in with me for a while and about divorcing."

I explained to her that it happened when Mark was living at home and running his business having people coming and going with calls night and day. He had no consideration for anyone and I was feeling so stressed that I was afraid for my health. I told Roy that either Mark had to move out or I did. I knew I could not accomplish getting Mark out of the house alone, that I needed Roy's support. Though he felt the stress less than I as he was away most of the time that Mark was operating, he did support me. That was the first time in twenty-four years that we were alone. It was wonderful for us both and we were sorry that we had not had him move out sooner. As I talked Beth continued to relax and the lines of tension in her face disappeared.

She went on, "Mark was so completely oblivious to other people's feelings, and to the stress he was causing by his life style. He had no appreciation that you were nice enough to let him live home and run his business. And he was so good at manipulating Dad. He seemed to get a wedge in between you." She laughed, reluctant to voice her next thought, "It's like Dad might choose Mark over you. I don't know that he would have. He let it go so far, like he wasn't able or willing to see what Mark was doing to the two of you. He accused you of being too critical or too sensitive."

We talked about some childhood memories, how it was for her as a little girl and how she sees her parents now that she is a parent. Then she went on to talk about her father more, "I've seen it take a real toll on Dad – he's aged. His face is not relaxed. He gets angry easier. He looks angry all of the time, just looks tired. Those two or three years when Mark was so bad, in and out of jail and on the street and in the hospital, there was so much pressure. Then you had all the problems that had to be handled regarding his painting business and the people he had working with and for him. It must have been hard to deal with the people who came to you to right the wrongs they said Mark had done them or the unfinished contracts you had to deal with."

We spoke of the people that came and went, how unstable many of them were, bringing additional pain and stress to our lives. I had thought we had protected our children from the magnitude of those problems only to find that Beth was aware of more than I had imagined.

I was feeling saturated and wished to end. I asked, "How are you feeling now that we've talked? Relieved that finally I can listen?"

She did not answer my question, but said, "Through the years I talked with my friends, trying to explain what has happened to Mark. At the same time I kept up on him, got involved with his living with us for a while knowing the things he had done, the trouble he'd caused, seeing the patterns. As I continued talking with my friends and getting their feedback, I've come to realize that he is permanently ill." Her voice broke, "I no longer hope. If he were going to live out his life like this, I wish he would die. But the tragedy is that he won't. He will continue just as he is now.

"Since Mark's illness I've lost a lot of faith in the psychiatric field. I think that they only can help you with mild neurosis, or pretty normal people that have life problems. For the serious things it just seems that there is still no answer."

Beth was far from finished, "You know for a while Mark was better on lithium but it didn't last. You have to have the discipline to keep taking the drug. It's as though the schizophrenia takes over every so often, throws him out of whack and then he messes up all over again. I know it's like the schizophrenia takes him out of choice. He really hears those voices he says he hears. It's real for him. His world is different from ours. One time I asked him if he understood what he put you and Dad through. He didn't know what I was talking about. Until recently that made me angry. Now I realize he just didn't get it. When he was oblivious to other people's feelings, I thought he was conceited and narcissistic, but now I think he was incapable of seeing beyond himself. It was as if he was emotionally stuck in the world of a three or four year old where the world revolves around him.

"I know it was hard for you to turn Mark away when he was hungry or had no place to go. It was hard to explain that to my friends, too. Coming from a Christian point of view, it is hard to do what you did, refuse to shelter him when he was no longer able to manage. I agreed with you that it would be wrong to bail him out of situations that he got himself into. I thought if he was ever going to get better or learn, you had to give up on him and you did.

"Now, Mom, I'm not sure he ever had a choice. I wonder if it was his destiny to become mentally ill at the time he did. Maybe his time clock ran out like our friend's mother with Huntington's Chorea. It just set in on her. She had no warning or no choice. Maybe that's the way it was for Mark. If he had taken a different path or made other choices, he would still have ended up as he did. Like it was predestined.

"Oh, another thing, I was showing someone the pictures of Mark and Paul and when I told her where Mark was, she asked me if we had ever considered demonic possession and exorcism?"

"As a matter of fact, I did wonder about it at times." I said.

"Mom, you don't mean it! I always thought that was some of that cultish stuff. I'm surprised you thought about it."

"There's a minister in our synod that spoke to me about doing something with Mark in that vein. We never got around to seriously consider it as we never got hold of Mark long enough to arrange anything. Mark was hard to pin down. About the time I would set something up, he would have been picked up and taken to jail or have gone off on some other tangent.

"Dad and I were talking about this recently," I said and he said, 'You know by the time we were eighteen or so, we would not have dreamed that our parents were responsible for our problems nor for taking care of them, regardless of what those problems would be. We knew that our problems were beyond their power to solve and that we had to work them out, whether it was relationships or illness. In the same way, I think that Mark may expect less from us than we expect from ourselves regarding him," I finished.

I looked at my watch. "It looks like it's time to pick up Jennie. Maybe we could finish up. Looks like we could go on for a long time. So many things to say that we have not taken time or had the courage to talk about." I stood up.

"There's still a little time. I have a few more things to say." Beth glanced at the clock and stretched. Then she went on, "All my childhood, I thought we were a very lucky family, that we were really blessed. I felt that way all the way up to college and my marriage. We would hear of families that had tragedies. I just thought we were really lucky and then things began to touch us closer and closer as your mother died and Dad's Mom died and then Mark cracked up. That was the very worst. Now I know that sometime in my life, with my family, we're going to be touched. No one is immune to tragedy. I just pray that we can live to old age and see our children grow up to lead productive lives."

I picked up my keys, "Me, too. Let's pick up Jennie." I could hardly wait to hold and hug our four-year old grandchild.

When I finished writing up our talk, I asked Beth to review it and make any corrections or additions that she thought important. She kept the manuscript for days and spent considerable time and effort looking over the material and thinking about what she had said. She added this:

"Sometimes it's scary knowing our family history of mental illness and I occasionally recognize some of Mark's irrational obsessive traits manifested in my own behavior. I have a tendency for exaggeration and am excessive as well as obsessive in spending money, eating, hobbies, and so on. And I am frequently oblivious to the feelings of others. I have an erratic nature and I often lack focus or direction. I get extremely sidetracked and rarely complete projects in a reasonable length of time.

"Being aware of these traits in myself has, at times, made me wonder if I will succumb to the same fate as my brother. But, at the same time, I have a very stubborn, strong part to my nature that will probably help me to stay sane.

"Talking about this and recalling the relationship we had with Mark has been very helpful to me in recognizing my own weaknesses as well as strengths. I've also recognized some patterns and feelings that have been getting in the way of a more positive relationship with my sister, Deborah. Maybe at last I can resolve what I never understood before. Taking the time to really stop and think about Mark, and how all of us interacted with him, has allowed me to recognize some things about myself that will help me in my other relationships."

Beth summed it up well when she said, "Now that I am older and I see things from a different perspective, I have more compassion for Mark living in his tragic hell. I no longer feel the anger and resentment I once felt. However, if the same pattern were to occur and he would begin to draw us all back into his web of deception and we were not strong enough to help or rescue him, I am sure these feelings would resurface. But this time I will come from a much better understanding and possibly the anger and frustration will be directed more appropriately. Maybe we have learned enough not to let his illness disrupt our lives as much as it did in the past. At least I hope so!"

Chapter XI.

I had not planned to talk with Roy individually about his experience since I was confident that I knew what it was like for him. We had talked endlessly through the years about what had happened. Roy frequently had said that we needed to talk less about our situation, dreams, fears and thoughts about Mark. I was surprised one day when he approached me and asked, "Don't you want to hear my side?"

I was glad for his willingness to participate and to be represented in my book. Perhaps I would find, as I had discovered talking with the children, there was a lot of Roy's experience that I didn't know. This would give us an opportunity to review new information as well. We agreed upon a time to talk.

When we sat down, Roy was silent. He looked so uncomfortable that I wondered if he would change his mind. I felt my own resistance to reliving the past with him. As he shifted in his chair and fumbled with the crease in his pants, I studied his expression. The lines in his taut face revealed how much he had aged.

Since words do not come easily for him, I waited to give him time to marshal his thoughts. His feelings were so easily aroused when it came to Mark that I suspected he was reluctant to begin. Once we began, however, he opened up easily. When he did not volunteer to speak, I finally opened.

"What was it like for you that night of my fiftieth birthday when Mark came in, threw himself down, beat and hammered on the floor as he screamed, 'I'm going down to Los Angeles to see Barbara Streisand!'"

Visibly startled by the stark picture I had described, Roy was silent as memories flooded in on him evoking the emotions of that night. He stammered as he attempted to verbalize coherently not only what he had felt then but was feeling now.

"I was shook and upset. Never had I seen him so wild and crazy. It was terrifying to see such a total collapse in our son. He was so completely overcome by his unconscious that he had lost all ego control. From my work in the hospital so many years, I recognized a psychotic break. Because I was seeing it in my own son, I wanted to deny and refute what I was seeing, rationalize it away. I wanted to think I was dreaming and that I would wake up. Everything happened so fast that I was stunned. I needed time to think and put things together, to make some order, and feel some control. There was a living breathing, person, our son, going crazy right before our eyes, and I couldn't do a thing about it."

Searching for words to further describe that day, Roy took a deep breath. It was his way of collecting himself and keeping calm. I watched him struggle to suppress his emotions while, at the same time, I urged myself to stay calm, to remember that we were talking about the past. I waited, hoping Roy would go on voluntarily.

He went on, "Though we canceled our dinner plans, two of our friends came over with the birthday cake. I would have preferred not to see anyone so soon after Mark left, when we were so shook up and confused. I was ashamed and embarrassed, felt vulnerable to having this family dilemma exposed so soon. I also felt really bad because it was your birthday—of all days for him to come by in that state! We had planned a nice celebration for you and then that happened."

Though it was still a sensitive issue for me, I wanted to know how Roy felt about my responsibility for Mark's illness due to my family history. We had talked about it in the early years. I asked, "When we realized that Mark was mentally ill, that this was not something that was treatable for a cure, did you blame me because of my Dad?"

"It's hard to remember. So much of it is a blur. I can't say when I felt what. There was a mix of feelings and, yes, sometimes I did blame you." He brushed over his admission of blame. "But I blamed myself, too. I questioned myself over and over about what I had done and not done. You accused me of not being firm enough and I blamed you." He was emphatic when he said, "But we also supported one another very much. When you were up, you would encourage me and when you were despondent, I would cheer and encourage you. As I recall we utilized our skills around the grieving process and getting our emotions out. I think you would agree with me."

I did not take Roy's blaming to heart as much as he thought I might, and I wished only to hear the truth. Sometimes he was overprotective of me and would soften his answers. It took him years to discover how tough I am. Though I felt some guilt at being the one who carried the mental illness in my family, over time I felt less and less guilt. I knew it was something beyond my control as much as the cancer in his family is beyond his.

Roy became restless. While he said he was willing to talk to me, now I sensed his increasing discomfort and wondered how long he would stay with me. We were at our country house where he spent hours enjoying work in the garden. He looked longingly out the window. I waited. He was quiet.

"What has it been like for you these ten years since Mark's breakdown?" I asked.

He thought a while and then said, "It's been like a prolonged grief, like a subterranean stream that surfaces from time to time. It's always there."

Roy sighed. "Like when you have some sadness or some tears and you work through it and then it goes underground for a while and surfaces again later. When you're busy, you don't think about it and when there's not much interaction with Mark, you aren't aware of any feelings but with the slightest trigger it is there again, surfacing in the same old way, resulting in sadness and depression.

"When he was out in the community there was always so much agitation and so many troublesome things to handle that the pot was always boiling. I had to handle some awfully stressful situations, like the time I was called to the "Y" where he was living and he was in a wild state at the YMCA entrance, threatening the police with a knife.

"The police were there with people I knew. Besides having the crisis to handle, there was the shame and humiliation of the chaos caused by my son. All of it happening right out on the public sidewalk at a main intersection. And he was in city jails where I knew people in the police department, and of course, he even appeared in the court of one of our friends who was a judge. That was all pretty humiliating. There were so many people in public life who knew us that had to deal with him.

"There was a sense in which I felt supported, I also felt a deep sense of failure, embarrassment and self-blame. I judged myself severely and thought others must judge me similarly.

"Everything was contaminated. Work-related problems probably seemed more serious than they were. I had so much feeling about myself, Mark and you, of all of us, that I don't know where one thing began and another left off."

When he paused, I remembered how confused I had been, and hurt, when friends pulled away from us. I, too, had felt ambivalent, excessively emotional and at my wits end so many times. Until he told me, it was not apparent that he had felt those similar feelings. He was known in the family to be the calm one and better at keeping things to himself. As he exposed his vulnerability, I felt a surge of love and affection for him.

"There was one time when he came into the office upset and hyperactive. I was with a client. One of the other counselors was with a client. Mark got the rooms mixed up and he pounded on Keith's door. We all came out and it was a horrendous scene, trying to calm him down, handle our clients and explain it away as best we could. It was a mess."

I sighed, "Gosh, I'm tired of talking about Mark, aren't you?"

"For sure. Maybe you have some particular questions you want to address," Roy said.

"Yes, I do. What responsibility, as a parent, do you feel for Mark now?" l asked.

"I feel pretty clear about that. I want to keep the relationship and visit him sometimes, not often, though that causes me some guilt. I don't feel stuck anymore and I don't have to blame myself as I did. I think of him now as an adult, no longer a child, dependent. His life is beyond my power to influence and I no longer feel responsible to seek ways to help him. When I became an adult, I didn't hold my parents responsible for me. Thinking that way has helped me to let him go. I have come to see that I am helpless to change his situation anyway. I am relieved to know I did my best and so did you.

"Another thing is that your self esteem is affected when there is mental illness in the family. Mine was severely challenged when Mark collapsed."

"You had risen high in your profession so you had a long way to fall," I said.

"I guess you could put it that way. I had felt pretty good about my work and career and what I did for a livelihood was the very thing that was called into question. When Mark became ill, it was a severe blow, still is. Though I never doubted my competency as a counselor and was able to separate what was happening with him and the problems people brought to therapy. I have had some pretty disturbed clients that I have been able to help over time. I suppose that was why it was so hard to accept that I was unable to help my own son.

"I saw so many people on the psychiatric ward at the hospital and there was always a lot of argument about whether their illness was functional, biological or genetic. Those years we traced so much to the early years. It certainly damaged my self-esteem when the popular theory was that parents were pretty much to blame for the mental illness of their children. I believed it and so did you."

He was right. I strongly supported "the family did it" theory. It was not until I saw the similarity between my son's illness and what I had seen in my father as a child, that I began to consider the possibility that Mark's illness might have a genetic origin.

He went on, "Anyway, to continue about how it was for me as a counselor. Work was positive. It was a place where I could function and it was something I could do.

"Nothing we did for Mark was effective. We were so helpless there. All we experienced for our efforts was frustration. No, even though my self-esteem was badly battered, I felt competent at work. Over the months and years, I came to have more empathy for people like us, families that suffered what we were suffering. I had a new appreciation for that whole realm of families coping with mental illness."

Each time we talked Roy insisted that Mark's fate might have been avoided if he had been diagnosed differently. I knew he felt strongly about the diagnosis. Though I had once shared his opinion, I no longer agreed with him. I had come to believe that nothing could have altered Mark's fate. Our dissenting opinions were beside the point. I wanted to hear Roy out.

He said, "He was treated early for schizophrenia when I think he was manic-depressive. For many years, he was very manic in his behavior and did not exhibit depressive symptoms. When he became psychotic, the doctors were deceived because they did not see depression until later. They refused to listen to your theory that Mark's busyness was his way of running away from his depressive side. They didn't give us credit for knowing as much as we knew and did not take our opinions seriously. I could be pretty angry about that, if I thought about it too much.

"They used all the wrong medications and Mark was so allergic to them that he nearly died. They refused to try lithium, though we all urged them to do so from the very beginning. When they did finally try lithium, we had some positive results.

Mark did very well when he was on the drug but by then it was probably too late as the physical damage from all the wrong drugs had taken their toll. I think Mark was a victim of the times and of medical experimentation. He was such a difficult case that he frustrated the doctors immensely. I think they tried their best. However, by the time lithium was used there had been so much damage to his system that his symptoms were very confusing to diagnose. They could never get control of the symptoms after he had been treated for so long with the damaging drugs."

We discussed at length the theory of diagnosis as we attempted to make sense out of what had happened to Mark. Either we believed that if we could finally understand what had happened, the situation would be easier to endure, or our struggling with ideas kept our feelings of anguish at bay.

Roy's voice became soft, "It has been so discouraging, so chronic and ungiving!

For some people, the ineffectiveness of medicine and psychiatry is blatant. In this case, the hopelessness of trying to get help for our son made it very hard. In general, in most things if you make enough effort, you get some results. This has been such an unyielding and discouraging situation. And yet, because of it, I believe that I have more capacity for deep feeling now. I think of Kahill Gibran in THE PROPHET, where he speaks of Joy and Sorrow, saying that the deeper that sorrow carves into your being, the more joy you can contain. He goes on, 'Is not the cup that holds your wine the very cup that was burned in the potter's oven?' And, of course, in the case of our son, where he says, 'When you are sorrowful, look again in your heart and you shall see that in truth you are weeping for that which has been your delight.' Mark was a delight to us, our first son, so bright, so quick, energetic, full of ideas, never mind that he was a challenge. We must not forget the delight we had in him, too. And that we had him for many years before we lost him. That is what we want to remember, isn't it?"

We had been enmeshed in negativity so long, we had almost lost sight of the good things about having Mark for our son. I blessed the poets and artists who called us back to witness to the wholeness of life. It is easy to become so narrowly focused on ourselves, our small world, that when life becomes difficult, we lose sight of the World.

I was satisfied with our discussion and thought about ending, when Roy asked, "Any more questions?"

I thought for a while then said, "Yes, there is something else, about me. Did you sometimes think about how it was for me having grown up with mental illness and then facing it again as a parent?"

"Of course, I've always felt sympathy for you. That's another aspect of the unyieldingness of it. To have it repeat again in our family!" When his voice broke, I felt his love and sympathy. There was no need to go on yet Roy was not finished.

"I can also feel some anger. I can be angry with God that He could be so cruel. There are a lot of cruel things in this world, the wars in other lands and all the things that are going on all around us. Sometimes it is hard to accept it all, much less understand it. But back to you. I have felt great sympathy for the struggles you have had through the years. Not always in the form of pain, but just the hard stuff of facing your family dragon and confronting it. I have admired your courage and persistence. I guess your saving grace was your determination to make it and you have. Yes, I have a better appreciation for what those scenes might have been like for you as a child now that we have had our son doing some of the things you talked about when you told me about your father."

My husband's sincere expression of my struggles and his sympathy for me were reward for those hard years. I was understood, admired and loved by another. What more could anyone want? Overcome with immense gratitude for our life together, in that moment I felt like a lucky woman.

Because I saw Roy continue to grieve our loss, I had not realized how much he had let go of Mark; that he no longer felt he had to keep trying to save him. I was glad when he said he did not want to visit Mark as regularly as we had. We had both seen, for a long time, that it did not make an appreciable difference to Mark and it had made a considerable difference to us. We were miserable for days following our visits.

Because Roy had been successful, as a therapist, for many years helping others with their problems, I knew how difficult and frustrating it had been for him to discover, despite his expertise and knowledge, no matter what he did for Mark, he was unable to help or save him. I hoped that he would understand and accept that this failure was not an issue of competency or self-esteem but rather a fact of his fallibility as a human being.

We have matured and come to accept that life doesn't always fit our pictures of the way we would like it to be. When it does not, we want to meet the challenges it presents with all our courage, wisdom and love.

Chapter XII.

After talking with each of the family members individually, I decided I would get the five of us together when our second daughter, Deborah, came home for a visit in the summer. When I told the family, they agreed that they would like to get together to talk about Mark. They all knew, by now, that I was writing a book about our experiences with him. Although they had agreed willingly enough, when it came to getting together, one difficulty after another arose. The first date we made was canceled when Paul had to work late. The second time we had agreed upon, the arrangements Beth had made for her children failed. Our time was running out for Deborah's visit would soon end. When we finally met for dinner, which I had prepared, there were still Deborah's two children to accommodate. The last hurdle we faced was getting them to bed, a task not easily accomplished as they basked in the attention of a doting family.

When the children were in bed and we gathered in the living room, it was the first time since Mark's breakdown that we had been together with just our immediate family. We were all noticeably nervous. There was no question that they expected me to take charge. Even Roy, who so easily assumed the role of leader, sat back and waited. The eyes of the children and Roy were all on me. As I looked at our three adult children, I saw them, as a group, for the first time, as peers.

My blunt opening remark was intended to startle them. I said, "I suggest that the five of us now think of ourselves as a family and close ranks."

I saw Beth's surprised reaction. Before she could respond, Paul said, "This doesn't seem like our family. Too relaxed. Not enough chaos." His light tone covered his reaction.

"We had that at dinner with the little ones," I replied. Maybe we would need some time to shift from dinner banter to somber conversation. I did not intervene when he began making light talk about the chaos the children caused.

I had learned in leading groups that often a member of the group would facilitate movement if the leader allowed time before intervening. When that happened the result was sometimes startling.

"About closing ranks without Mark. That makes me sad," Beth said. "Me, too," Deborah chimed in.

"No mad Mark? No, we can't leave out mad Mark," Paul said. Ignoring Paul's distracting remark I went on. I spoke to them about coming to terms with the fact that Mark would no longer be around and that, though he was one of us in the past, we might just as well think of ourselves as a family without him. Since I had slowly come to this conclusion and Roy and I had discussed it, I expected that the children would agree with this logical conclusion. While Beth and Deborah agreed, Paul argued.

"With Mark you can't depend on anything. His illness is cyclical. He is up and down. Just when you write him off, he'll change. You can't count on anything with him." Paul's voice was tense with an edge. The last thing any of us wanted was that Mark should be with us these days. It sounded like Paul feared that our hard days with Mark were not over.

Deborah volunteered thoughts of her experience, "There were periods when I liked him, certain times when we shared interests. We went camping and we shared books with one another. It was brief. He diverted all of the focus of the family on himself. He was so competitive."

"He was always wanting to be as good as I even though I was three years older and would be better at everything I did until high school when he surpassed me. It was such a frustration. I don't think I ever liked him," Beth added.

As they conversed, even though they reviewed many of the incidents that they had talked about with me, I kept quiet. They had not heard one another voice these things. When we had been together in the past, either the subject of Mark was too painful, there would be too many of us around, there was a crisis to handle or we were often busy or involved with our grandchildren. None of us wanted to deal with the problems around Mark when he wasn't physically present. We wanted to forget about him, consequently we had not ever really talked about these things in depth before. As I listened, I could understand why the children felt so much resentment toward their brother. It made me sad when I realized how much resentment had been focused on Mark over the years since his breakdown.

Deborah said she felt mostly sad about Mark. Beth admitted that she used to be angry with him but now she pities him. Then Beth asked Paul how it was for him.

He replied, "I don't think about him. It's too depressing to think about him, so I don't. He drove us crazy when he lived with us. He's a clown, never thinks of anyone but himself." Paul's anger made it hard to be aware of any other feelings he might have. We could all hear how angry he was. No one challenged him or reacted. It is what I had hoped would happen but I had not realized how mature our three other children had become until that moment.

Roy, who is prone to listen more than to speak, began to talk about Mark's lack of sensitivity to others and how it affected us all. Paul shared frustration after frustration, none of it new to either Roy or me but it was probably good for the women to hear what he had been through. We let him vent his anger.

"He was totally uncontrollable," Paul said. "Nothing ever stopped him. He was always scheming and wheeling and dealing, no respect for authority, he had no ability to hold a job." Paul stopped and looked around the room.

When no one argued with him or reacted, Paul's need to vent his anger subsided. The tension lifted in the room. For a while we all sat quietly.

Not only had our children matured, Roy and I, too, had gone through some growing changes. As Mark's parents, in the past, we would have become defensive and taken Paul's outburst as criticism of us. We would have intervened to comfort and to help Paul understand so that he would feel better, not be able to hear him out. Now we sat quietly while Paul vented his anger uninhibited. Beth and Deborah, too, were able to allow for his strong reactions without becoming involved with him at the expense of losing sight of their own experience. Though both of the women had expressed the same kind of anger and frustration in the past, they had each gone beyond anger to compassion.

Beth spoke, "I don't remember having any love for Mark. Did you, Deborah?"

"I felt close, though sometimes distant, too, because Mark replaced me with Mom and Dad as the next kid. Of course that has nothing to do with the way he was. That was a more natural resentment of a child."

Paul chimed in and the three of them discussed their feelings for one another, mostly positive, and for Mark, quite negative. When we asked Paul about some of the early experiences that we all remembered about his and Mark's relationship, he could not remember many of the incidents, which we cited.

"I don't remember the times when you left us to get ourselves off to school, when you went to your class before us, Mom. We were probably more independent of you than you realized. You worried about our hurting each other uselessly."

"I won't argue with that," I said. "Worry is useless. Generally the thing we worry about isn't the one that happens anyway. It is always something else."

We went on with "do you remember" as we dredged up old memories, hurts and pains. There would be years of pain to process before we would remember the good times.

"Do you remember how I used to beat Mark up for you when you were little?" Beth asked.

Paul smiled. "You protected me from Mark? That seems funny now." He stretched and yawned. Now a six-foot man, he knows he can take care of himself.

Since Roy had been silent throughout the interchange, I drew him in. "Roy will you explain the identified patient theory for us?" I asked.

He said, "The identified patient theory comes out of the family systems theory in which one member of the family is identified as the disturbed or sick member and functions to distract the parents and other children away from their own personal unresolved conflicts. The identified patient becomes the focus of an unfair amount of the normal negativity that is generated in families. He draws to him most of the negativity. The presence of this member keeps the family system in a functional balance even though it is an unhealthy one for the identified member and makes him the scapegoat. The cost of this way of functioning in the family, according to this theory, is that the problem person may become schizophrenic."

When Roy paused, I went on, "And since we both ascribed to this theory, we saw Mark early as the identified person in our family. We worked very hard to handle our own personal problems so that he would not bear the burden of our conflicts. We soon saw how Mark would come between us and how easily we would become involved in fights with one another over his behavior. But, of course, when he got sick, we blamed ourselves for we thought that we had learned and applied this theory too late to help Mark."

I was surprised that Deborah, who is a child psychologist now, did not challenge what we were saying. The children listened attentively as Roy went on, "I was trained in the psychoanalytic model and I tried to understand Mark from the functional and dynamic aspect, which would lay the blame on us as parents and me as a father. I didn't see you, Ellie, as the carrier of the disease, yet that was always there, your family history. It could not be ignored entirely and it did give us something concrete on which to pin his illness."

Paul leaned forward in his chair to speak. Ignoring him I added, "Dad and I have felt like we were responsible for Mark's illness. We believed that if we had been wiser and had been successful in applying what we knew, that we could have saved Mark. We had a lot of support for that viewpoint. Most everyone in the mental health community laid the blame on the mother, father or both."

"You can't be serious," Paul was incredulous. "Mark was impossible. He turned everything around. You could do nothing with him. He would do terrible things and then you would end up feeling guilty. He would want to use your phone in the middle of the night. If you would tell him to get out he would say you were mean and that he would let you use his phone. He would bring a taxi to the house and ask you to pay for it. You would feel guilty if you didn't pay the driver and guilty if you did because then Mark would have won another point for his crazy behavior, get by with it.

"You can't be serious, that you were to blame. Mark created his own chaos. He made so many messes everywhere he went. He had a phenomenal capacity for creating havoc. One Christmas I got several phone calls asking for him. People were ready to lynch him for all the ripping off he had done. I got a lot of calls because I was the only other Futscher in the phone book. Mom and Dad had gotten an unlisted number."

Beth looked at her father, "You must have gotten sick of hearing what Mark had done, not only from others but also from us," she said.

Paul was not finished. He was agitated now. "He was difficult but not crazy as a kid. What upset me was how you never said no to him, Dad. Everything focused on Mark's projects."

Roy explained, "He just had so many things going all the time. I got pulled into them and then there was very little energy left for you other children. That summer he started boat building, he was at me to help him the moment I came from work."

"Oh, Dad, it wasn't only that summer, it was all the time. He took all of your time and I got very little attention from you," Paul argued.

Apparently feeling no need to defend himself, Roy was silent. This was the first time Paul had directly confronted his father with the resentment he had harbored toward him and had expressed to me and to his sisters.

Beth spoke up softly. "You know when he stole you the most? When he became ill. You were totally involved cleaning up his messes, trying to get him help, and you were not available to us emotionally because you were so strung out."

Deborah was crying when she said, "It is sad that he consumed so much from so many people. I think you always thought if you gave enough he would make it. What else could you do? I would do the same for my kid."

Using the story of the prodigal son from Scripture, I said, "Because the three of you were doing fine, we did not have to attend you. Mark was the 'prodigal' that we missed and wanted back in the fold. We always hoped and prayed that enough love and the right care would pull him through."

I began to appreciate how deeply involved Paul had been with Mark as he continued to talk. He went on, "Mark would go off the deep end, head for the stars, wheeling and dealing, getting crazier and crazier. He would not sleep for weeks on end and become more and more hyperactive until you felt thoroughly distraught around him. Broke, is all I can say. He is broken and there is nothing you can do about it." He was emphatic, as if that were the final word according to Paul.

It was not his final word. Paul went on to state firmly and dogmatically, "Mark's responsible for how his life turned out. I don't go with this genetic theory. He made choices over and over that led him to where he is now."

There was no need for Roy or me to defend or explain. Deborah was quick to refute his dogmatic pronouncements as she cited case after case where outrageous behavior preceded the onset of a debilitating disease such as Huntington's Chorea and Alzheimer's Disease. She said, "Mark was out of control and could have done no differently than he did."

Paul would not back down. "I don't buy that he had no control. I lived with him and saw him and his behavior for years. You didn't."

I looked at Roy and wondered what he was thinking. I thought of the many people, like Paul, who feel even more strongly critical of the mentally ill. I felt an overwhelming sadness for the victims of this terrible fate.

Roy's thoughtful intervention claimed everyone's attention. Paul, who had been concerned that his father would not participate with the discussion if things became heated, looked at Roy as Roy began to speak.

"Mark made a lot of immoral choices and each time he made one it became easier to make the next one until it became easier and easier and things became worse and worse for him. His life style was totally manipulative, really sick. He would feel guilty yet keep repeating the same behavior. It all converged to drive him crazy. It is hard to say where and how it started but you are right about the behavior being immoral."

"He's not an innocent victim. He is responsible for his illness", Paul stated firmly.

Speaking as a psychologist, Deborah said, "When people make bad choices over and over, like steal and cheat, you will see them ten years later and realize that the early behavior was the beginning of a severely degenerative disease. Schizophrenia is like that."

Paul, who has probably read little or nothing in the field of psychology, said, "Not necessarily. I disagree. You still have to wonder if one causes the other."

Both Paul and Deborah, specialists in their field, are easily able to articulate their opinions. It was interesting to listen to their arguments but when I saw that it was a fruitless discussion that would lead nowhere, I decided to cut in to bring us back to talking about ourselves. I thought of the lines from the poem by St. John of the Cross, "I Came into the Unknown" "Scholars argue long but never leave the ground. Their knowledge always fails the source to understand...."

"Well," I said, "we can all be glad for the peace we are enjoying now that Mark is in the hospital."

"No problem there!" Paul responded. "There was no one more destructive than Mark. He was the king of destruction. There are others more violent but no one more destructive."

Roy told the children a number of destructive things that Mark had done around our house. Beth urged me to put it all in the book, "Don't leave anything out, Mom. People will never understand unless you're willing to tell it all."

"No matter what you say or how you tell it, no one who has not been through it would understand. There is no way you could communicate to anyone what it was really like. I don't see how you are going to write a book about us. You have a tough assignment for yourself, Mom," Paul said.

For the first time, we heard from Paul what we had known ourselves: how difficult these years had been for him. Recognizing his need to talk, Beth and Deborah listened patiently as he vented his stored up frustrations.

They talked about what they thought I should include in the book.

"You have to tell about Daffy Duck," Paul said. "Mark loved Daffy Duck, the troublemaker. He always cracked up over the duck's antics. It was as if he himself was that character."

"Well, we always said of Mark that he kept the pat boiling, that there was never a dull moment when he was around," I added.

Before speaking, Deborah looked at Paul to be sure he was finished then said, "Dad, earlier I got on your case because you gave Mark all the attention. However, now I don't think there was anything else you could have done. He was such a shaky kid. You tried to give enough to anchor him. He sure did take it out of you. Even regular kids need so much. If you have one like Mark, it is bad news. Paul, you had grandpa. He gave you a lot. We, Beth and I, missed out more than you. I'm so glad he's locked up."

Did Paul hear what Deborah had said? I hoped it would sink in, that they, too, felt the deprivation he felt and that Roy could have done no differently. It was my fervent hope that Paul could drop his burden of resentment.

Deborah laughed and said, "Let's put Mark aside and go after each other."

"Wait a minute," I said. "Is there anything good we can say about Mark?"

"It's hard, Mom. But he was interesting when we were younger and when he was nice he was pretty good," Paul softened a little.

Beth said, "He liked my kids. He loved Allie especially and gave her her first pair of ballet slippers."

Roy and I did not have to say anything. We had both known this boy from his birth and we had countless memories of a healthy happy loving child. This was not the time to talk about that. The others wouldn't have heard anyway.

Roy asked Deborah what she thought about the diagnosis, given what she now knew and what she had learned from her years of private practice. She could be no more decisive than anyone else that has tried to make sense out of this insidious disease. Paul's next question was fraught with anxiety.

"Do you think this is going to run its course and that he is going to get out? Isn't it cyclical as much as degenerative? Is this time for good or will he be out in three years down the line. He was clear and normal the last time we visited, Dad. Is this for good or not?"

"No one knows for sure but if you look at his record, he has never really been in remission in ten years. In the last three he has deteriorated badly. Though Mom and Dad were hopeful when the shock treatments began and he made some progress, he soon relapsed. He is so hard to treat because he is allergic to neuroleptics, which they use to control the disease.

It looks pretty hopeless to me. But then no one knows, of course," Deborah said.

Reassured with Deborah's response, Paul did not press the question of whether or not Mark would be released again. Instead he asked, "Just what does shock treatment do?" He looked to Deborah who answered.

"It disrupts all the electrical transmission system in the body. This gives temporary relief from the voices, which makes the patient subdued and almost normal sometimes. You can imagine it would have a dramatic effect for it is like being struck with a thunderbolt. The memory loss that occurs provides additional relief to the patient. The long-term damage is hard to evaluate, as there is much we don't know yet about the brain. With Mark, it is almost impossible to assess the damage from the shock treatment as there appears to be so much damage already from all the medications he has had."

Roy, who has seen many patients who have had shock treatment the years he worked in a hospital said, "None of us can appreciate what a hell it is to hear those voices in the head day and night. But we can guess. Mark lived with that for years before he finally submitted to shock treatment. He must have been at the end of his endurance to finally agree to it. When we saw how much relief he had, we were glad, even if it has not lasted."

"I published a research project with a colleague. I received many letters from families of patients like Mark. There were so many stories as bad and many worse than ours. I don't think Mark is that unusual at all in the population of the mentally ill," Deborah told us.

Though that knowledge did not comfort me appreciably, I felt less alone than I had for years because our family had finally sat down to talk together. This seemed like a good place to end. Roy and I took our leave of the children. They stayed on and talked for hours. I fell asleep to the sound of their laughter.

Chapter XIII.

Like the disease it names schizophrenia is a discordant and cruel word. For those of us who hear it applied to our family, it is the most frightening word in our language. That it is more common than the public realizes makes it no more acceptable to those who learn that the illness is in their family. It occupies more hospital beds than any other disease. On any day there are 600,000 people being treated. Each year another 100,000 are diagnosed as schizophrenic. If you take the numbers who are hidden, undiagnosed, unrecognized and not acknowledged, the number increases. Yet the disease remains closeted. Families with a schizophrenic member often hide the fact because they fear the judgment of others and they think they will be shunned if people know that there is a mentally ill member in the family. Their fears are not always unfounded.

Three quarters of those with schizophrenia develop the disease between the ages of sixteen and twenty-five. A family that one day seemed to have only normal problems are suddenly catapulted into a foreign world, terrifying and crisis-filled. Dreams and hopes for the victim vanish and families are torn apart. It is hardly any mystery that by the time the experts get around to studying the family, the mother and sometimes the siblings are in such a state that they are diagnosed as schizophrenic-type parent or sibling.

The disease can take several courses. One group of sufferers may spontaneously recover, often rapidly, after the disease hits. The middle two groups range from those who can hold a job while taking low dosages of drugs to those who exhibit symptoms but can live in the community with some supervision. The final group is the one that does not respond well to any treatment and are the ones that may commit suicide. When the disease strikes young people, its early symptoms may be confused with adolescent rebellion or drug use. The dress, behavior and music of the youth of the sixties looked extreme and bizarre to the conservative professional at that time.

In an early study in the twentieth century in which workers diagnosed family members as either schizophrenic or not, they found that approximately 4% of the parents and about 8% of the siblings of schizophrenics had been diagnosed as schizophrenic. About 10% of the children of couples in whom one parent was schizophrenic were themselves schizophrenic.

Acute forms of schizophrenia tend to disappear with the passage of time with or without treatment. These people prior to their illness were psychologically and socially relatively adjusted. Their illness tends to have some attributes of psychoses produced by chemicals and brain dysfunction, such as confusion; is often characterized by changes in mood, either depression or mania; and is often precipitated by a major psychological set back such as the loss of a loved one or a profound disappointment. Persons going through divorce or who lose a spouse experience this kind of confusion and mood swings and sometimes think they are going crazy.

The history of the chronic schizophrenic is quite different. The onset is often gradual and insidious. A slow transformation of the personality seems to take place, which may be dismissed as unimportant until an acute flare-up occurs that may require hospitalization. The person may then have persistent hallucinations and delusions, which are often only reduced through drug therapy. Thought disorder, disorganization, impaired planning, poor judgment, irrationality, and peculiarity may persist. While the patient is being restrained in the hospital he or she may be talking about going to work or school. Their thinking is so confused that they cannot see the relationship between their state and their being in the hospital.

Improvement is usually only partial. The patients' lives are generally characterized by inept social graces and often by repeated hospitalizations. Many chronic schizophrenics have been deviant children or rebellious rule-breakers not unlike other juvenile delinquents. When acute episodes repeat over and over, some patients develop a chronic psychosis, which becomes a lifetime illness.

Schizophrenia makes the brain process information inaccurately. The disorder is not a psychological one. The overt symptoms are delusions, hallucinations or illogical thought associations, to less obvious symptoms, such as confusion, apathy and withdrawal. Schizophrenia is sometimes used interchangeably with psychosis, which simply means "not in touch with reality."

The American Schizophrenic Association gives a list of "danger signs" to alert families. They say to watch for unaccountable changes in personality, confusion, memory loss, insomnia and disturbances in seeing, hearing, smelling and touching. While this is helpful in recognizing that something is wrong, it is not guaranteed an accurate diagnosis. Often if the family sees the signs, they refuse to believe anything is wrong and look the other way until it becomes impossible to ignore the seriousness of the problem. Families who are naive about drug problems may think their family member has been taking drugs.

Symptoms, which schizophrenics may have, are also common to other brain diseases such as brain tumors and temporal lobe epilepsy. Those that are common to both are

1) alterations of the senses.

2) altered sense of self (may have grandiose ideas about their abilities.)

3) delusions and hallucinations.

4) inability to sort and synthesize sensations and an inability to respond in an appropriate manner.

5) changes in emotions

6) Changes in behavior.

No single symptom is essential to the diagnosis of schizophrenia. Many true schizophrenics have other symptoms but never have delusions or hallucinations. Schizophrenia is the most expensive of our chronic diseases because about the time a person would become a contributing member of society, the disease strikes and the patient becomes dependent upon society. Almost no family could bear the cost of this disease. Despite the outrageous cost to society, until recently, the illness was largely avoided and not talked about. For each schizophrenic patient there is $14 spent per year on research, compared with $61 per year per victim of multiple sclerosis, $300 per year per cancer patient and $1,000 per year per victim of muscular dystrophy, according to figures compiled by Dr. E. Fuller Torrey, author of *Surviving Schizophrenia*.

There have been two intellectual and therapeutic movements to attempt to help to alleviate the misery caused by mental illness. The first includes various versions of the psychodynamic theory, which are now being carefully studied as limitations of this theory have become known in the mental health community. The second movement is the resurgence of the theory that there are organic and genetic factors causing mental illness, particularly schizophrenia.

Interpersonal factors seem to be important elements in the understanding of schizophrenia. It does not seem to occur in those who have even for a short time made a definitely satisfactory adjustment to the opposite sex. While this finding does not indict the family where children learn interpersonal relationship skills, it does seem to support the psychodynamic theory. I used to worry when Mark could not make or maintain satisfactory relationships with girls. We used to talk about it with him. Though he wanted desperately to relate to girls in high school, he did not succeed.

European psychiatrists of the early century assumed that schizophrenia was hereditary while European psychoanalysts believed the disorder to be untreatable with psychotherapy. Americans did not share this belief and began to treat schizophrenics with psychotherapy. The theory of parent blaming was furthered. Recent discoveries encourage a change in the thinking of professionals as patients have responded to drug therapy and failed to respond to psychotherapy.

To prove the environmental theory one study found that both spouses were caught up in their own personality difficulties, which were aggravated to the point of desperation. In seven of eight families studied, the husband had little prestige in the home. Imperviousness to the feelings of others is characteristic of many parents of schizophrenics. In the troubled marriage the children may become more vulnerable, torn between conflicting attachments and loyalties, to schizophrenia. That patients become psychotic when their communication breaks down corroborates the theory of family responsibility. It has been hypothesized that the schizophrenic patient is more prone to withdraw from others because his reality testing mechanism is shaky, having been raised with irrational and distorted facts that makes the environment confusing.

For years theorists blamed parents, especially mothers, for their schizophrenic children. They were said to be women who needed and used their sons to give their lives meaning. One psychologist, claimed that malevolent mothering caused their children's illness. His article was published in a well-known professional magazine. Bruno Bettelheim's parent blaming was downright cruel. Parent blaming was popular in the early fifties and continued for a number of years. Paula Kaplan and Ian Hall-McCorquedale of Toronto did a study of mother-blaming, published in the "American Journal of Orthopsychiatry," July 1985. There was a "professional ideology that crystallized in the 1950's in which the causation of all psychopathology, from simple behavior problems to juvenile delinquency to schizophrenia was laid at the doorstep of the mother." The National Alliance for the Mentally Ill (NAMI) discovered that "education" tapes, available to relatives of those with various illnesses, included tapes on schizophrenia, which conformed to the "family did it" theory.

During the parent-blaming era, dedicated therapists worked on removing victims from their environment—going so far as to take them into their own homes, a classic "rescue" pattern. Many therapists believed the Gregory Bateson double-bind theory, popular in the sixties, which proposes that it will be difficult for a person to stay sane when he is exposed repeatedly to double bind behavior, i.e. a person (the mother, in the case of the schizophrenic) conveys to the child that he should do something and at the same time communicates in a non-verbal way that he should not do that same thing, or even worse, that he should do something contrary to the first request. Brought up in such an environment, Bateson maintained that a child would become schizophrenic.

With the research that has been done in the last decade it is less common for the family to be told that they caused the schizophrenia. It still happens. There is a gap between information and its application. Doctors trained in years past believe the old theories in which they were trained. Because families feel guilty and blame themselves, it is easy to see how they would accept the family-blaming theory when they encounter a doctor or other professionals who abide by that theory.

While theories are changing in the circles of mental health professionals and involved families, the American public still believes that schizophrenia is not a disease—it's a weakness in character. There are some psychiatrists who still maintain that schizophrenia is not a disease but a way of thinking and behaving. Many people think the schizophrenic is one who does not want to take responsibility and that he is malingering. We, too, used to think our son was lazy, as he would often accuse himself when he could not motivate himself to act. For a long time we all thought that he could help himself more than he did. When someone as close as we to the disease is misled, it is not surprising that there are gaps in the public's understanding and acceptance of schizophrenia as a disease that calls for treatment by the professional community.

Because schizophrenia is now so prevalent, there has been increased interest in finding causes and cures. After the movement to de-institutionalize hospital patients, which began in the 1960's, many schizophrenics lived at home after their hospitalizations. Families were forced to become case workers, nurses, and doctors, roles they didn't know how to play, and to assume responsibility for adult children when it was time for these children to be out of the home. When the children would normally be separating from parents, they were suddenly totally dependent upon them creating even further problems and making it almost impossible to define illness separate from dependency and interdependency between parents and children. This situation set off intensive interest in schizophrenia among families who were becoming burdened beyond their tolerance level with this hopeless disease. Because of their unending frustrations, these families began talking, studying and learning what was available to learn about the disease and in 1977 an organization for families came into being. In 1987 the American Schizophrenic Association celebrated its tenth year. About the same time the National Alliance for the Mentally Ill, (NAMI) another organization for the support of families was formed. Families came together in mutual concerns for the mentally ill and to support one another.

The body of knowledge regarding the possible cause and treatment of schizophrenia has grown the last ten years. At this time scientists cannot agree on whether the disease is genetic, passed from parent to child, bio-chemical, caused by some defect in the hormonal system, caused by a virus which attacks some and not others, a failure of the autoimmune system to fight that suspected virus or a combination of all these factors with the family dynamic causes/factors thrown in.

There are some recent studies that found that complications such as prolonged labor, interacting with hereditary influence, increase the risk of schizophrenia, which suggests that oxygen deprivation might be a cause.

To add to the accumulating body of theories, there is now some evidence that the time of year that the child is born might influence the susceptibility to schizophrenia. Twenty studies during the past four decades have shown a consistent 5% to 15%, increase in schizophrenic births during the winter and spring months in comparison with the general population. One study showed a greater incidence of schizophrenia among children whose fathers had died during the mother's pregnancy.

The viral theory continues to have some prominence, and it has been proposed that the increased incidence of the illness in lower socioeconomic groups may be related to greater susceptibility to infectious processes as a result of deficiencies in the home.

Studies of psychosis in children indicate that many of such children have either symptoms or past histories suggesting damage to the brain. A study of soldiers who suffered wartime brain injuries found that twenty years later the men developed schizophrenia at five times the rate of soldiers who escaped such injury.

Although it is possible that psychological or social influences might affect the way the symptoms manifest, at present there is no reason to believe that those factors can or do cause chronic schizophrenia. At the same time, if in some instances of any disease, it is found that there is a genetic component, it does not follow that all cases are genetically transmitted. By the same reasoning, if it is not genetically transmitted, it does not necessarily follow that it is psychologically caused. Individuals experience many biological health problems in the course of their lives that may affect their normal functioning, i.e., the onset of diabetes late in a person's life can alter their life style and emotional adjustment drastically. It has been found that persons undergoing major surgery sometimes suffer severe emotional shock and are placed, for a time, in the psychiatric unit of a hospital.

Psychiatric illness that is genetically transmitted must have biological basis whether through genes, vulnerability to viral infections or other abnormality of the immune system, or through some cause as yet unknown.

Differences among people may make them more or less resistant to life traumas. For resilient or less vulnerable people, things seem to bother them less than the more vulnerable ones. Those may become mentally ill with very little exposure to disturbing experiences and traumas, whether in the form of childhood problems or adult stress. Some people may survive an extremely pathological childhood and succumb to mental illness if stress in adult life persists over too long a period of time or is very severe. Still others may endure the same degree of hardship and yet retain their mental stability. When the stress around our son continued relentlessly for years, I marveled that my mental health was good. When, after seven years my system did react when I got cancer, the first in the family to have cancer, I was convinced that the stress had taken its toll in this physical form in my body.

Two possibilities of psychological vulnerability are first, biologically connected psychological illness can sometimes be prevented by changing circumstances of the person. The person might be removed from an atmosphere that increases and aggravates the stress to an environment that is quiet and stable. Second, some medications may be used as protective measures. In the argument against the psychodynamic model, the effectiveness of individual or group psychotherapy as the major treatment has not been proved. When our son was in the hospital in the early period of his illness, his brother and sister went to the hospital to participate in a group therapy process to help their brother. Mark did not attend the group or if he did, he wandered away or did not participate.

There has been little progress in determining the cause of the disease. There have been discouragingly few new or significant breakthroughs with medications or other forms of treatment. While we better understand the role of neurotransmitters in producing crazy behavior, this knowledge has not made for substantial improvement in the life of many patients. We are still a long way from finding causes of schizophrenia. Unfortunately, we cannot yet talk about cure.

Though treatment is difficult, and progress slow in finding cause and cure, with the development of neuroleptics or anti-psychotic drugs that came to the market in the early 1950's, the symptoms can be controlled in some patients. Patients who are hallucinating, agitated and delusional get some relief from the drugs. There is evidence that anti-psychotics can and do keep some schizophrenics from relapsing. They do little to change negative symptoms such as social withdrawal and lack of motivation. At one time in Mark's treatment program when he appeared to be well, the doctor told us, "Mark is completely recovered except he lacks motivation." He was soon to prove that without motivation, one is not well and that it is impossible to function for long in the world.

Medication is the preferred treatment for some psychiatric illnesses. For severe psychosis and schizophrenia, psychological treatment is considered to be an adjunct to medication, not the other way around. Those psychotherapists who in the fifties had faith in psychoanalysis for severely psychotic patients have had to change their thinking after years of frustration with treating these patients without medication.

It has been found that medication is a must if symptoms are to be relieved, and in this sense an individual may be dependent on medication for his well-being. It is only when some of the symptoms are relieved that there is any hope of helping the patient to gain insight into his illness and the necessary motivation to cooperate in controlling the symptoms.

The dependency on medication is not considered addictive. Contrary to the claim that drugs are overused, it is more likely that the major psychiatric medications are probably under used. Studies of symptomatic volunteers illustrate the extent of the untreated sufferers. Many of the homeless people who walk the streets of our cities the country over are the untreated victims of severe mental illness. Some of these would respond to medication if they were to come under treatment and the quality of their lives greatly enhanced.

There is much experimentation going on in research around mental illness. The breakthrough in drug therapy, while effective in controlling symptoms, has done nothing to enlighten us about causes. There is no evidence that if we had done something different with Mark, that he would not have had a breakdown. Children raised in the same family do not all succumb to the same illnesses, obviously. Twins raised apart have been found to have similar physical and mental problems. Does this fact support the argument for genetics as the cause? While we want to remain positive and hopeful, the current research does not encourage hope. Diagnosis remains a problem. Schizophrenia can be confused with bipolar disorder, amphetamine psychosis and temporal lobe epilepsy. Several things called schizophrenia turn out to be something else. One researcher is known to have said, "If the patient was cured of schizophrenia, it probably was not schizophrenia," reminding us that there is no cure for this dread disease and giving us cause to be even less hopeful.

The review of literature reveals that we are still some long way from a breakthrough regarding cause and cure of schizophrenia and other mental illness. The best we can hope for is that we shall all survive in a way that the quality of life of those around us that are not ill in our families will be as good as we can make it for ourselves and each other as we support one another and our ill family members.

Fortunately, there are now some resources for families and friends of the mentally ill that did not exist in the early years of our family crisis. Both the American Schizophrenia Association and the National Alliance for the Mentally Ill are well-established effective organizations that help to educate and support families. There is more public awareness of the problems that this population faces and increasing sympathy and support. Things are moving and changing and we wish to keep the momentum.

Chapter IX.

I have heard that love, not time, is the healer. I have had both. I have had love. I have had years! How much time do I need and how much love? I am impatient that I continue to grieve, that my days are frequently full of sadness for Mark. His fate stalks me and I think about him too much. With a death, it is possible to finish the grief process. There is no finish with the situation that we live with daily.

Time has not healed. It sets up ambushes at unexpected turns along the way.

Recently I was driving through Berkeley on a warm spring day. I was feeling positive, almost happy. As I approached a school, I glanced over at the playground. A blonde boy about twelve stood alone looking so like Mark that tears blinded me as I remembered a time when that could have been our healthy son standing on the playground. I had to stop the car to have a good cry before I could attend to my tasks of the day. The rest of that day a heavy cloud followed me, and I was despondent where a moment before that scene I was happy. Where is the healing, the resolution, for my grief?

It seems that what has happened to Mark will never fade from my memory and that I shall never stop crying for him. When I am alone and silence surrounds me will I be able to think of other things? Or will I have to always invent distractions and activities to still the grim memories of those years and of his present fate? Will I be able to push it away when no duty or activity presses upon me? I thought that writing the account of these years might bring healing. One morning recently I woke to the realization that I had not thought of Mark for a number of days nor had I dreamed of him for some weeks. I was encouraged thinking that I now could be more objective about Mark's illness. Then I had a call from the hospital that Mark had lost thirty-five pounds and was being transferred to the medical unit of the hospital to be checked out. It seems he was starving himself.

Though I knew he had been in restraints and was barely rational, I decided to go see him. When I saw his gaunt face, I hardly recognized him. He was severely psychotic, talking to himself. Still he recognized me and cried when I held him. I sat with him for some time, caressing his hand and trying to let his senseless chatter go in one ear and out the other. I thought I was doing well. When I left him I was so sad I could barely muster energy to drive home. As long as he lives I feel I must take time to make contact with him. Though everyone he has known has long stopped visiting him, Roy and I cannot bring ourselves to desert him. I want him to know that he is not forgotten and that he is loved. It is true that you can never give enough to a schizophrenic. They are insatiable in their need for love. You could give them love twenty-four hours a day and still it would not get through to effect a change. These children have a bottomless well of needs that no one can satisfy.

I am content that I am able to get through to Mark even a little. The staff is always glad to see me and presses me to visit more often. They become discouraged at their inability to reach Mark.

If I could live my life over, have the years back again, knowing what I know now, would I be more understanding and loving? I would know that Mark was disabled and could not help himself, that he had inadequate controls. I wonder if I would be more patient and less frustrated and bewildered. I'm sure I would. Sitting here at my desk I can imagine myself more patient and loving. Given the behavior that we had to deal with, I doubt that knowing would change my ability to cope. We gave and gave to Mark. I cannot fault myself for neglecting him. No matter. None of the above would change his fate. He would still have the dread disease, schizophrenia, for which there is no cure.

Now that I have lived through ten years of Mark being diagnosed a schizophrenic, I am glad that I was protected as much as I was from my father's illness. Though I used to think it was wise to let children know the hard things as well as the easy things in life, I now think it might be good to shield our children as much as possible and as long as possible from the hard things. Life problems impinge upon them soon enough without our intervention. When Allie, our granddaughter, was three she was with me when Mark broke all the windows. She lived through that terror with me. When he came to the door months later and I carried her to the door to answer, she jumped down from my arms, backed all the way through the front hall and to the end of the kitchen behind the hall and pleaded, "Don't come in, don't come in." I was crushed. Mark loved her and would not ever have wanted to cause her anguish or fear. She was too young to have that experience. I wish she had not been there. The more mature the child, the better his chance of assimilating and making sense out of any experience. Perhaps one day she and I will talk about that episode which by now she has suppressed into unconsciousness.

We cannot protect our children from earthquakes, murders, war, and sometimes broken windows. We are powerless in those areas that do not respect children's rights. Those things come to us uninvited, ready or not. Children touched too young are not given wisdom but more easily acquire distrust, despair and self-depreciation. Our family is lucky that we did not have to deal with Mark's illness early in his or our life. Roy and I would have been much less able to cope when we were younger and more idealistic about life. I am grateful that the other three children were well on their way to adulthood when Mark broke down. They were all three already out of the home.

When Mark had his first psychotic episode, I was hopeful for his recovery when his father said, "When a symptom is severe and sudden, often the recovery is as dramatic and not far behind."

Comforted by those words spoken by a man who had worked in hospitals all his life, I suppressed my own nagging fears and doubts, desperate to have faith that Mark would recover. It is said that faith begins where understanding ceases. I never stopped trying to understand and my faith was never strong that Mark would recover. I had lived through a childhood of hoping my father would recover and lived to see those hopes dashed as my father had episode after episode of manic-depression which took him in and out of the mental hospital.

How I tried to believe in Mark's recovery. Friends and family would tell me to hope and pray, that they were praying for his recovery, too. Just recently I had a letter from a well-meaning friend from the Alliance for the Mentally Ill, who said that she believed in miracles and was praying with confidence that Mark will recover. I accepted her good wishes in the spirit with which she gave them. She cares. Though I assured her that I, too, believe in miracles, I had no confidence that Mark's healing would be one of the miracles I should live to witness. She urged me not to give up hope. It was a familiar refrain, "Don't give up hope."

One day I realized that hoping was a way of hanging on and that regardless of what anyone said, letting go of Mark was imperative for me if I were going to have a life with my husband and other children. Too much energy was going into this one son. I was still pouring my all into this bottomless pit, using all my personal resources in a hopeless cause. I like what the poet T.S. Eliot said in a poem, "Wait without hope for hope would be hope for the wrong thing." Wait. I would not be hopeful or hopeless but would wait. And while waiting, I would go on with my life.

I no longer feel angry with anything or anyone. Even as I fumed and raged at God, I knew that I was only venting my feelings. Though in a childish way I still wanted to be special, I knew God had not picked me out for punishment or for favor. My raging and conversations were so childish I would have been embarrassed to tell anyone how I felt. I was glad to have this mystical sounding board. Even as I fumed, I felt that I had a friend, that God had not deserted me. Because I so easily dialogued with God, I knew I had not given up on Him. At the same time God wasn't giving up on me as I struggled with my faith or lack of it. I wrote in my journal one morning, "I will do Your will, God. Reveal it to me and give me grace, wisdom and sense to abide by it no matter how I feel about it." There was a part of me that always knew I was loved and watched over by God.

Though I am not a theologian, I have been interested in theological questions all my life. I knew that God wasn't doing anything to me, that He wasn't going to change His laws to accommodate me. Nor did I believe that God was pouring on the suffering because I was strong enough to bear it, as sometimes people would say in their attempt to comfort me, "God doesn't give you more than you can bear." My image of God became fluid, changing from day to day. Rigid concepts that I had held shattered before new ones could form. I held fast to my prayer and meditation discipline despite doubts that nagged. The discipline was a centering ritual giving me steadiness through each day.

When the world gets to be too much for me and the problems that confront me appear insoluble, I feel bitter and resentful over what life has given or withheld from me. I question the purpose of my life, whether what I do or don't do will make a difference in the world to anyone. I feel like giving up, and I can understand Mark's despair and his many feeble and futile attempts to end his life.

It is a tenuous thread that holds us all in balance between our will to live and our will to die, our sick selves and our healthy selves. I can feel when I am depressed how fragile that thread is. It broke too soon for Mark. He fell off the life side into the death side without dying.

I am not so fragile. I catch myself when I am in a negative phase, wake myself up to remember that I do not have to concern myself with making a difference in the "World" but only with my "world". Certain that there I can make a difference, I go on with faith and courage.

Happiness is not the only purpose of my life. Though I am not sure what else my life was given me for, I know that given life, I must live. I have lived, fully and richly. I have had an overwhelming sense of being loved by God in many ways, times and places. It is irrelevant that I have been happy or unhappy. Everyone, at one time or another, has those emotions. Each of us experiences the gamut of human emotions or has the capacity to do so. Some of us don't experience as deeply as others and some of us don't even recognize what emotions we are experiencing. Through our common humanity, we share similar emotions throughout our life span. Depending upon the way we put life together, the decisions we make, the genes we inherited, the sex we are, and much more, some of us have more happiness and others more misery.

Happiness and satisfaction in life come more from accepting things as they are, letting things be, than from the kinds of things that happen to us or that we make happen. It has a lot more to do with attitudes than events. Happiness is also enhanced by a willingness and ability to change and a faith that it is possible to do so.

Some things we cannot change, such as the genes we inherit. Those are givens. If we are to change what we can, the burden rests upon the individual. We cannot look to someone else to do the changing. If transformation is to occur in any situation in life, it will come about because I am willing to be the channel.

The call to wholeness, to love, to holiness, is what is crucial. I must do whatever it takes to clear from my life the accumulated dross. I must learn to contain the opposites within myself in the context of love, regardless of how trying or difficult the problems. I need to learn how to hold my sorrow and my joy in balance.

I must take care of my body and spirit in order to maintain the energy it takes to overcome the forces of darkness that threaten me with isolation and loneliness. Once I have set the goal then all the forces within me converge to assist me to achieve it. Though I make mistakes, or take the wrong turn, I must continue to take a step at a time trusting my correction mechanism to intervene when I go too far astray.

One of my lifetime goals has been that I shall have a loving supportive family. In faith I have set my mind to that goal and moved in the direction of that possibility. I have had to push through resistances at times to keep that goal in mind. Through the years, as we have grown and changed, we have become a loving supportive family. We can turn to one another in time of need.

I have lived my life with integrity and lived by my ideals. When I have failed I have learned how to forgive myself and go on to try again. I see an amazing perfection about the pattern of my life.

I don't understand how Mark's illness fits into my goals, ideals and dreams. Yet, sometimes in life that which is the most threatening and negative is that which in the end is what saves a situation or brings about the needed change. Perhaps all of us needed changing in our family. Certainly I have.

I have learned that I must have the courage to face life, to face the most threatening situations without feeling guilty or ashamed when they occur. I must bear humiliation, shame and weakness and go down into that which I most fear. Out of my willingness to confront the darkness, from somewhere beyond all conscious expectations, there may be a flicker of light, a stream of energy that will probably not produce a heroine but will at least provide the inspiration for me to continue keeping on, to take one more step in the direction of life, love and truth.

I do not have all the pieces to the puzzle, which is my life, but then my life is not over. As I discover additional pieces that fit into the puzzle, my picture grows rich in hues, intensity and beauty.

About the Author

Eleanor is the mother of four children and grandmother of seven. She is an active member of a Lutheran Church. She keeps fit with tennis, swimming, housework and gardening. She divides her time between Jenner by the Sea and Oakland, California, where she lives with her husband, Roy.

Bibliography

Atkinson, Jacqueline M., SCHIZOPHRENIA, Turnstone Press, Wellingborough, Northamptonshire, 1985

Cope, Louis, R. M.D., F.A.C.P. IS IT ALL IN YOUR MIND?, The Naylor Co. Book Pub. of the Southwest, San Antonio, Texas, 1972.

Dearth, Nona, Labenski, Barbara, Mott, Elizabeth, Pellegrini, Lillian. FAMILIES HELPING FAMILIES, W.W. Norton & Co., N.Y. London, 1986

Gibran, Kahill, THE PROPHET, Alfred Knoff, N,Y. 1968

Kharitidi, Olga, M.D. ENTERING THE CIRCLE, Harper Collins Pub., 10 East 53rd St. New York, N.Y. 10022, 1996

Laing, R.D., SELF AND OTHERS, Pantheon Books, Random House, Inc. N.Y. 1961

Lidz, Theodore, M.D. & Fleck, Stephen, M.D. (in collaboration with others), SCHIZOPHRENIA AND THE FAMILY, International Universities Press, Inc. N.Y. 1985

North, Carol, M.D., WELCOME SILENCE, Simon & Schuster, N.Y. 1987

Parker, Beulah, A MINGLED YARN, New Haven and London, Yale University Press, 1972

Peck, M. Scott, M.D. THE ROAD LESS TRAVELED, Simon Schuster, Rockefeller Center, 1230 Avenue of the Americas, New York, N.Y. 10020, 1978

Shapiro, Sue A., Ph.D., CONTEMPORARY THEORIES OF SCHIZO-PHRENIA, McGraw-Hill Book Co., N.Y., St. Louis, San Francisco, 1981

Siegler, Miriam and Osmond, Humphry, MODELS OF MADNESS, MODELS OF MEDICINE, MacMillan Pub. Co. Inc. N.Y. 1974

Sullivan, Harry Stack, M.D., SCHIZOPHRENIA and THE HUMAN PROCESS, W.W. Norton & Co. N.Y. 1974

Torrey, Fuller, E., M.D., SURVIVING SCHIZOPHRENIA, Harper & Row, Pub. N.Y., Cambridge, Philadelphia, San Francisco, London, Mexico City Sao Paulo, Singapore, Sydney, 1983

Walsh, Maryellen, SCHIZOPHRENIA, STRAIGHT TALK FOR FAMILY AND FRIENDS, William Morrow & Co., Inc. N,Y. 1985

Wender, Paul H., M.D. and Klein, Donald F., M.D., MIND, MOOD AND MEDICINE, Farrar Straus Giroux, N.Y. 1981

Wilson, Louise, THIS STRANGER, MY SON, G.P. Putnam'a, N.Y. 1968